STAY YOUNG
AND HEALTHY
THROUGH
INTERNAL CLEANSING

by
Millan Chessman

TABLE OF CONTENTS

ACKNOWLEDGMENTS

I want to thank William Saccoman, M.D., of El Cajon, California, who had confidence in me and allowed me to work out of his office, giving me my start in internal cleansing.

Thank you, Leslie Williams, President of the International Association for Colon therapy (IACT), for contributing your wisdom and research.

Also, thank you, Mike Wourms, author, for your help and direction in writing this book. It could not have been accomplished without you.

Finally, thank you, Joe DiLella, for your input, patience and love.

INTRODUCTION

What if you found out that a few minor adjustments to your diet and lifestyle, coupled with a simple, painless, and inexpensive office procedure, could help you not only live longer, but maintain ultimate health, vigor, and mental acuity into your nineties and beyond?

Would you take the necessary steps to enjoy life unimpaired, especially if these steps were low-cost, low-tech, drug-free, and non-strenuous? Does this sound too good to be true?

NO!

Chances are, your doctor will not tell you how to take these steps. He or she probably does not know about them.

These pages reveal a little-known secret to health. Because of complicated, toxic, and oftentimes unsuccessful medical practices today in the United States, this secret to health has become hidden.

Wouldn't it be great not to always rely on expensive doctors, high-tech equipment, drugs, and hospitals?

A healthy person does not need medical help. The answer to ultimate youthfulness and health that so many have found is a simple, painless procedure. It is called internal cleansing.

No Longer Taboo

"Yuck!" "Disgusting!"

These are typical responses to any mention of the human colon and its affiliations. Even in modern times, the lower part of the digestive system is a difficult subject to discuss. We can speak with ease about what goes into the mouth and into the stomach, but conversation stops there. Food is digested through the stomach and small intestine, but what happens from that point on is usually ignored.

If we want to be healthier, live longer, and improve our outlook, we need to examine the vital core of our well-being. This core is finally becoming obvious to more than an elite few who have known for years that a key to health is in the colon.

My Own Start In Internal cleansing

My first internal-cleansing was twenty-three years ago. When I saw what came out of my young, beautiful, and perfect body, I was shocked. I thought, "If I contain such garbage, then other people must also!"

I read every health, nutrition, and internal cleansing book I could get my hands on. My bowels moved once every four or five days. I knew this was not optimal, but my doctor said it was "normal" for me.

You may have heard that yourself.

My personal and professional research and experience have taught me emphatically it is not normal for me, or anybody else, to walk around carrying rotting pounds of sewage in my body for weeks and even years.

Some health practitioners believe that because the average American could have five to fifteen pounds of fecal matter in the colon, havoc is played with the body's balance of intake and elimination. This is the reason behind many potbellies. Granted, fat is there, but excess stool is there as well.

This, in fact, makes us walking cesspools.

Our condition is an open invitation to disease and sickness. I am concerned and want the public to become aware of this health problem.

This is why this book is being written.

Life-changing Program

I have worked in San Diego as a certified colon hydrotherapist since 1982. My experience, after administering over seventeen thousand internal cleansing treatments and relieving much pain and anguish, has compelled me to publicize the need for individuals to start internal cleansing programs. Such programs will truly change lives.

When my clients see all kinds of rotten matter come out of their bodies, they experience what I call a "new awakening," and their lives are never the same again.

When I first established my internal cleansing practice, I was under the supervision of William Saccoman, M.D.. My approach has been different from many other colon hydrotherapists.

Whereas internal cleansing is the beginning and end of most practices, my services include "the Cadillac of all cleansing programs": a complete program of providing information on the many benefits of juicing and eating correctly.

Providing a complete cleansing program is possible through either a juice fast or diet modification. This provides the start to continue a client's new found health.

I attended the Arizona Holistic Institute, where I studied anatomy, physiology, nutrition, and health. While there, I also learned how the digestive system interacts with all other body systems, what are the important psychological implications, and how to administer internal cleansing.

Terms for this procedure are entero lavage, colonic, colon therapy or internal cleansing. All mean internal bowel cleansing. I am correctly referred to as a colon hydrotherapist.

I read every book possible about fasting, internal cleansing, and enemas. But most of my experience comes from years of performing colon hydrotherapy.

Because few schools offer necessary detailed training and internships, actual training is currently limited. This is largely a result of the medical establishment's stubborn refusal to accept internal cleansing; therefore, the American Medical Association will not recognize it, let alone establish standardized curriculums at accredited professional teaching and training facilities. A person who cuts hair must be licensed in all states except Florida, yet a colon hydrotherapist cannot become licensed!

This therapy is seldom mentioned in modern medical literature, and what is cited is overwhelmingly negative. Without factual basis, the literature presents internal cleansing as useless and

7

unfounded. Its overarching importance to health is grossly overlooked.

A Changing Health Field

Modern medicine has remarkably low cure rates for the diseases and conditions it treats. Dissatisfied patients are seeking more effective and less expensive answers to their physical ailments. Alternatives to costly procedures offer more wholistic approaches to wellness. These changes challenge the American Medical Association and result in better health.

A Grateful Woman's Story

One client wrote me:

My father died suddenly in bed three weeks before his ninety-ninth birthday. He was very active and had many colon cleansing sessions during his lifetime.

Years ago, I had a few colon cleansing sessions and then forgot about them until recently. A friend told me about her colon hydrotherapist and what the therapy had done for her. I am sure Our Lord worked this out to help me regain better health.

I have had several sessions, and now I truly have a new lease on life.

Three years ago, I was put on oxygen eighteen hours a day because I have chronic obstructive pulmonary disease (COPD). I was married for 26 years to a smoker, although I never smoked. I have been diagnosed with asthma and emphysema as a result of the second-hand smoke.

About four months ago, I broke my left shoulder. Since then, to help me breathe, I have increased my dose of Ventolyn Spray medication to every three hours. Every four hours is the maximum dosage. However, since my third session, my breathing has improved. This past week I have gone four, five, and even six hours between Ventolyn doses. It is truly wonderful to sleep six hours without interruption.

My energy level increases daily, and I feel so much more alive. The junk and toxins shed during my colon cleansing sessions reveal why I have not been in good health. It is unbelievable all that was in my intestines - undoubtedly for many years - since I was constipated a good part of my life.

Anyone who has ever been constipated would greatly benefit from internal cleansing. Some people believe it can add ten years to your life, and I concur heartily.

Dorothy M.

Internal Cleansing's Challenge

The challenge colon hydrotherapists face is at least threefold:

First, there is resistance from the AMA. Clients have stated internal cleansing provides both immediate health and longevity.

The practical evidence is abundant, yet the AMA requires repeatable results from standardized tests. Interestingly, such tests have never been conducted.

Without documented experimental and clinical results and thorough studies, the evidence for internal cleansing cannot be discredited.

The AMA may be revealing the medical industry's interest in maintaining the lucrative status quo of ill health; it is well known that some doctors maintain their high standards of living at the expense of unnecessary and unhealthy conditions of their dependent patients.

A healthy person means lost revenues for the medical establishment. Increased health means a lower demand for high-cost, high-tech "medicine."

Internal cleansing is low-cost, low-tech, yet time consuming. It can be administered by someone other than a fully licensed medical doctor, but we must no longer deny its effectiveness.

Second, I believe internal cleansing should be a standard office procedure with medical doctors, chiropractors, naturopaths and acupuncturists.

Third, and perhaps most important, is the challenge of people themselves. People need to take control of their bodies. Health conditions and decisions needed for staying young and fit are vitally important.

Someone else's scare tactics should not influence our health decisions. We should find health professionals who offer workable procedures. Time is too short to waste on treatments that do nothing but bring disease, suffering, and even premature death.

A Client Discovers Health

I recently went through an internal cleansing program, and my health improved! I was tired, my stomach ached and was bloated, and constipation was a problem.

My doctor recommended internal cleansing, so I did not waste any time getting started. The colon hydrotherapist guided me through the program. The more she explained to me, the more it made sense.

I feel as if for years I have been mistreating my body.

Now that I understand, I know many people out there suffer needlessly.

I feel great!

Kathy M.

Health and Longevity

We were not meant to suffer from preventable diseases. Evidence shows wise health habits can keep us physically fit, mentally alert, and healthy...well into old age.

Some people claim they would not want to live that long. However, dynamic health and vigor might change their minds!

Great health and longevity are not miracles waiting to be discovered by some scientist in the distant future.

This is for us today.

In the following pages, actual personal testimonies will describe the relief others received from pain and illness through internal cleansing programs. These testimonials were collected over the years from my own practice. I hope they, along with the information in this book, will reassure and inspire you to take charge of your life by taking charge of your health. This step will enable you to stay young and healthy through internal cleansing.

CHAPTER ONE

A HISTORY OF INTERNAL CLEANSING

Internal cleansing is an ancient health treatment. Historically, it has been used successfully to treat almost every condition imaginable. But today, orthodox medical opinion takes a dim view of internal cleansing. Even enemas are suspect, though for certain medical conditions and procedural preparations - colonoscopy, lower GI X-rays, prep for many surgeries, and childbirth - enemas must still be employed.

Origin of Colon Cleansing

Four-thousand-year-old Egyptian artifacts depict enema implements and their uses. One document, known as the Ebers Papyrus, a toxicological and medical text by priests circa 1552 B.C., describes the procedure of "colon lavage."

Egyptians credited colon cleansing's origin to a legendary bird, the sacred ibis. Stork-like, with a downward-curved bill, the sacred ibis was said to have invented colon cleansing when, it seemed, it injected water from its bill into its own bowel. Colon cleansing thus involved rectally infusing certain "aqueous substances" - there were then an array of usable solutions - into the large intestine.

Hippocrates and Galen

Hippocrates and Galen both used colon cleansing in their practices and taught others how to administer the procedure.

In 500 B.C., Hippocrates, the Greek father of modern medicine, used colon cleansing to bring fevers down. This remains a valid application.

Another Greek physician, Galen, also administered colon cleansing to his patients and wrote about its uses in 200 A.D.

Women Healers

J. Glenn Knox, D.C., states:

For thousands of years most health practitioners were actually midwives and "lay nurses." These medicine women, healers, the wise women of their tribes and villages, used colon cleansing and combined it with herbs and massages.

From observing their patients, these women knew the health benefits of a clean, unclogged digestive system. They rightly believed a toxic body caused many illnesses.

Dark Ages

Historically, colon cleansing has been used to purge the large intestine.

During the Dark Ages, the technique's greatest employments were to counteract poisons (which were the most popular ways to commit murder or assassination) and to fight disease. Identification of poisons, plaques, and food poisoning (from rotting meats and other foods) was almost impossible to determine, so colon cleansing was used extensively.

Though many kinds of colon cleansing were described and used for centuries, it was not until 1600 A.D. that a Dr. Pare distinguished between colon hydrotherapy and "the popular enema of the day."

After this, the course of colon cleansing proves harder to track. Perhaps because in our culture the subject is publicly taboo, records of internal cleansing in the last two hundred years are rare. Some records may be found under the headings of physical therapy or massage. These were the areas of application until turf wars with the medical profession removed those avenues of application.

Royal Cleansings

In Europe, colon cleansing was common, especially among royalty. In eighteenth century France, "enema stools" were as common as footstools. "Colon laundries" were even established in London.

Before refrigeration, food spoiled quickly. Rich, flavorful sauces and gravies enjoyed today were created in ancient times to mask the taste and odor of putrefying food. For the wealthy, who could afford meat on a regular basis, it was not unusual to follow dinner with a colon cleansing.

The drawing shows antique colonic equipment. The photo shows new safety and sterilization features that greatly improved efficacy of the treatment.

15

Technological Advances

Increased technological requirements in education changed the titles of the "players." The "hospitals," where patients were treated, became the proper "stage" for treatment. By the late 1800's, modern science rapidly grew in organized fields of study. These were initiated and taken over by men for religious reasons, prestige, dominance, control, and monetary gain. These men became the doctors, and the common midwife became the nurse.

Through the years, internal cleansing has undergone many changes.

No More Messy Procedures

Conventional medicine began to drop archaic, messy procedures, such as colon cleansing as practiced more than fifty years ago.

Today, however, we have modern equipment which provides the most sanitary procedures for this therapy. In the early days, doctors thought sterilization and sanitation had nothing to do with contamination.

In fact, washing hands for surgery in the 1800's was thought unnecessary, until Louis Pasteur and the Scottish surgeon Joseph Listur developed a cause and effect relationship between bacteria and systematic infections.

The Western world entered the age of surgery, medications, and pills with rejoicing and awe. Fantastic - no need for repugnant, time-consuming colon cleansing.

Just prescribe a pill - and keep your hands clean - to get rid of unwelcome diseases.

Flourishing a pen, a doctor would prescribe quick, painless oral medication, usually solving the patient's problem - at least for the short term.

Meanwhile, the value of clean bowels was slowly dismissed. After all, who wanted to spend time, with little financial reward, dealing with feces?

Into the 20th Century

As doctors gained power through medical breakthroughs, their services came at higher prices.

16

With the birth of the Industrial Age in the late 1800's, the art of medicine became a thriving enterprise, reflecting the success rate of many large-scale businesses and factories.

In the first decades of the 20th century, standardized accreditation requirements were instituted for medical schools. This reduced the number of approved medical teaching schools.

Consequently, the social and financial position of physicians increased.

Assigned to Nurses

While it was not unseemly for mothers or nurses to administer enemas; more and more doctors disdained performing the procedure. After all, why spend years learning the marvels of the human body only to end up dealing with feces and offensive odors from patients unable to hold water in their colons?

So, the enema bags and internal cleansing equipment (still used in most hospitals until the 1950's, though not standard procedure as in earlier times) were relegated to nurses. And later, as their rank, prestige, and level of education increased, doctors passed bowel treatment administration on to lower-ranking staff.

Internal cleansing Equipment

Well into the 1940's, colon cleansing in hospitals was standard practice. Keeping the patient's colon cleansed was the main duty of the attending nurses. Colon cleansing was ever-present, and patients received treatment in most hospital stays.

Colon cleansing equipment was kept busy. But that equipment left much to be desired in the way of modern hospital sanitation, safety, and convenience standards.

Dierken Therapeutic Apparatus

Dierken Therapeutic Apparatus is one of the oldest known types of colon cleansing equipment.

In 1940, this machine was a considerable improvement over other types. It had, its promoters pointed out, "the effect of promoting physiological peristalsis, and of working free the contents of the 'pockets' and diverticula."

The Dierken machine had "a glass percolator and all the necessary plumbing attachments, control valves, and special irrigation features compactly assembled within a stainless steel alloy frame."

Safe Equipment

Today we have state-of-the-art, safe equipment with sterilization features and highly trained, certified colon hydrotherapists. The medical community that once banned internal cleansing should now recognize and incorporate modern internal cleansing into any complete health program.

Tapeworm Discovered

Dear Millan:

Diagnosed as having two different types of amoebas, I came to you for help. After the thirteenth treatment, I passed a flat noodle-like substance. Laboratory analysis revealed it to be a beef tapeworm. My doctor had performed numerous tests on me, yet had not discovered this creature. Thank you for your help.

Anonymous

Character Requirements

Colon hydrotherapy is administered by a certified, trained colon hydrotherapist. The procedure requires no drugs. First, a small speculum is gently inserted by the client into the anal canal. To encourage peristalsis, water is slowly introduced until the need for evacuation is felt. The colon then eliminates the water along with the softened waste through a closed system.

Empathy for the patient is required. A sensitive therapist enables patients to relax. Kindness, gentleness, being soft-spoken, and caring for people are vital qualities in a colon hydrotherapist.

A colon hydrotherapist must discern the needs of the client. Therefore, the colon hydrotherapist must be a knowledgeable and skilled specialist.

Economics of Internal Cleansing

Internal cleansing sessions take forty-five minutes to one hour. Taking medication requires only a few seconds. Time is money.

Mercury Toxins

Today, some dentists are removing amalgams (mercury fillings) from teeth. This is important to good health and a detoxified body. Yet, because their bodies are autointoxicated, patients are not getting the full benefit of this procedure.

In Sweden, Dr. Crister Inged Malmstromon studied patients who had mercury amalgams removed. Interestingly, the subjects had not recovered from the symptoms of mercury toxicity.

Only after undergoing a detoxification program of internal cleansing were the poisons released.

Laboratory examinations on fecal matter removed during internal cleansing showed mercury toxins in old stool lodged in colon pockets. Following treatment, patients actually recovered from the mercury toxicity.

Another study discovered eighty-five percent of mercury toxins leave the body via the colon. In other words, an improperly functioning colon hinders mercury from passing. Ultimately, mercury implanted on colon walls absorbs back into the body.

An internal cleansing program is essential to the full recovery of a mercury-toxified body.

Amalgam removal is expensive; moreover, it does not thoroughly cleanse the body from toxins. Internal cleansing is relatively inexpensive, ranging from forty-five to seventy-five dollars a session, and includes the important procedure of a healthful implant.

Remember that, in my opinion, if you do not receive an implant with your internal cleansing, you are being seriously short-changed, since it is understood that anyone needing detoxification has imbalanced flora.

Beneficial Implant
The benefits of the friendly flora which is implanted into the colon are as follows: it balances the bacteria in the colon, sweetens the breath and rids the body of foul odors, creates digestive enzymes, effectively breaks down carbohydrates, controls candida, reduces bowel irritation, improves digestion and assimilation, manufactures abundant nutrients, reduces fermentation, maintains alkalinity and the necessary acidic condition of the colon, eliminates gas problems, raises the immune system, aids in production of lactose, and eliminates rashes from food. Flora Source, a manufacturer of friendly bacteria, states the following:

Mounting research continues to prove that the health and efficiency of the digestive system, and the immune system, depend on the complex interaction of "friendly" bacteria and balance in gastrointestinal ecology. Interaction of certain beneficial strains of bacterial cultures can aid in:

1. Maintaining balance during and after the use of antibiotics, chemotherapy, sulfa drugs and other harsh medication.

2. Relief and prevention of food sensitivities (including lactose intolerance), constipation, diarrhea, abdominal pain, bloating, gas, and digestive disorders.

3. Support for sufferers of candidia, Crohn's disease, and colitis.

4. Production of enzymes and B vitamins, and synthesis of essential nutrients, including vitamin K.

5. Calcium assimilation and hormonal balance.

6. Production of short chain fatty acids, supplying 5% to 10% of energy needs.

7. Control of enteric infections.

8. Re-establishment and maintenance of healthy vaginal flora.

20

9. *Beneficial effects on cholesterol.*
10. *Stimulation of the immune system.*
11. *Digestive support while traveling.*

It is amazing the difference one feels just making a few changes to improve one's health. For example, many people have never heard of friendly flora which promotes good health.

Many colon hydrotherapists use colon hydrotherapy equipment that has the capabilities of administering oxygen via the water that goes into the colon. Oxygen destroys parasites and worms and gets absorbed into the body as well. Our body needs oxygen for abundant health.

Remember, these implants get absorbed through the walls of the colon and ultimately into the bloodstream. In order to do its job, the implant should sit in the colon for at least ten minutes without eliminating.

Some hospitals, however, still give enemas. Even a minimally skilled aide can administer one. Time-consuming, potentially messy, and requiring certain cleanup preparations, the procedure is avoided whenever possible.

In general, professional colon hydrotherapy differs totally from and lacks the offensive stigma of enemas.

Thus, the economic tide turned from costly personnel's administration of colon cleansing. The result was, almost inevitably, that from 1970 to the present, the majority of the medical doctors stopped prescribing colon hydrotherapy and reduced the use of enemas. There was never any proof established that enemas were harmful or worthless. They were just not cost-effective.

Pharmaceuticals

Because of new products from burgeoning pharmaceutical companies, doctors began to discount colon cleansing as a legitimate and valuable medical practice.

In the 1920's, John D. Rockefeller invested millions of dollars in certain pharmaceutical companies and bought out some prestigious but floundering medical schools. Consequently, doctors learned to write out prescriptions, which the pharmaceutical companies filled with their products. As a result, current drugs and technology have all but replaced simple, natural, preventive health practices.

Until the 1970's, chiropractic clinics offering colon cleansing existed nationwide. Now, only a few remain. This is unfortunate, since adjustments stay longer when internal cleansing is included.

The decline in medically prescribed colon hydrotherapy has spurred an increase of independent colon hydrotherapists. These service an informed and often desperate public. Seeking relief, patients feel their doctors cannot alleviate ill conditions they may have.

A Relieved Client

I was a mess health-wise. First, I have been constipated and have suffered terrible gas all my life. Second, I have had hemorrhoids since childhood. Inexplicably, another serious problem developed: regular bouts of vomiting. Despite numerous tests, doctors were unable to help me.

I then started internal cleansing with Millan. She put me on a detoxifying diet of herbs, and I did a series of twelve colon hydrotherapy sessions.

My life changed: my bowels moved more regularly, my gas problem disappeared, my energy level increased, and I started exercising regularly and drinking a lot of water.

My hemorrhoids were not as uncomfortable as before, and my vomiting stopped.

Juanita

Certification

Very few institutions certify colon hydrotherapists. In California we have three state-licensed schools presently teaching colon hydrotherapy. Florida is one state that certifies licensed massage therapists in colon hydrotherapy. In fact, the American Colon Therapy Association (now known IACT) as recently as 1990 states:

Florida is presently the only state that requires the licensing of colon [hydro]therapists. A license must be obtained under the provisions of a massage license through the Department of Professional Regulation Board of Massage...

Florida has been licensing massage since 1943. It began licensing colon [hydro]therapy around 1949. Consequently after forty-one years of experience Florida can be considered the ultimate model for the rest of the country (Allred & Dobrow, 1990).

From 1950 to the present, the trend moved away from internal cleansing, and more internal cleansing was referred to outside specialists.

Among medical professionals in the last seventy years, internal cleansing's popularity has declined. Misconceptions about the physiology and the efficacy of the colon resulted in wrong advice. For instance, from the thirties until recently, some believed that two or three correctly administered colon therapies would sufficiently cleanse the body.

Today, we know this is not true. Unfortunately, this bogus perception contributed to the medical profession's dismissing internal cleansing as ineffective.

Dr. Norman Walker, one of the grandfathers of modern internal cleansing, wrote seven books on health and colonics. A personal friend who knew him quite well once told me that when Walker died in 1987 he was 109 years old. To this day, he is respected and honored by those in preventive health. Walker advocated colon cleansing - sometimes daily for six weeks. Generally, the usual recommendations are around ten sessions, including an herbal cleansing program with a modification of diet.

Successful Therapy Story

Julie's kidneys hurt so that she could barely walk or touch her back. Her urine stung,

23

and she had to push it out. After the second session, all pain went away. Amazingly, her back felt better.

She exercised more, drank more water, and was eating healthier. She had gone two weeks without bowel movements, and she had headaches every day. After a number of sessions, she had bowel movements regularly and no headaches. After the tenth session, she passed two white strands, one long and white, the other shorter, which a lab later determined to be worms. She was very sick, but afterwards she received another session which relieved her discomfort.

Proper Equipment

One thing doctors need to understand is how important it is that water enter the body very slowly. Water entering the colon too fast would stimulate peristalsis too soon and cause discomfort.

The only known cases of perforation of the colon occurred in hospitals and involved infants and mentally disturbed patients, with adults administering enemas - not colon hydrotherapy. These are the reasons professional internal cleansing equipment is superior to that of an enema. With proper equipment, the water temperature can be controlled and kept at a comfortable 90 to 105 degrees Fahrenheit.

Centenarians

Ripley's Believe It or Not states:

In 1993 a Mrs. Harriet Breedlove of Knoxville, Tennessee was cutting a new set of teeth at the age of 102. Mr. Thomas Gordon of Grand Rapids, Michigan, had his hair turn black at the age of 103. Daphne Travis of Atlanta, Georgia at the age of 108 years was hale and hearty and was cutting the third set of teeth. Her eyesight was improving and her hair, which was white as new wool for 50 years, was turning black again. George Washington Emerson of Newport, Maine, was cutting his

*third set of teeth at age 93 years. He says he is
not yet ready to retire; instead, he wants to go
into the chicken business. He has never been
sick except once with measles. He has never had
to wear glasses.*

An investigation of these folks reveals their
diet consisted mainly of vegetables, fruit, seeds,
nuts, and grains. Most were vegetarians, eating
these God-made foods.

Before the Great Flood, mentioned in the Bible,
people were vegetarians. After the flood, they had
to eat meat. Now, the average life span is seventy
years instead of eight hundred.

Individually, we have little control over our
environment. We breathe impure air consisting of
carbon dioxide and monoxide. Our insides are
poisoned. Our air loses precious oxygen from
heaters. The list goes on and on.

*Many of these centenarians worked until
they died. A few daily walked a good distance,*
Ripley continues.

*An interesting case was a Chinese man
who lived to be 254 years old. Documentation
verified his age. His lifelong diet was mostly
vegetables, especially herbs and roots. His
name was Lin Ching Wan.*

*Another centenarian lived to 160. His
birth certificate proved it. Interestingly, this
man fathered his thirty-sixth child at age
ninety-six. In later years he grew black hair
and cut new teeth.*

Enema Solutions

In the early 1900's, gastroenterologists
sometimes recommended enema solutions of soap
suds, salt, molasses, soda, vinegar, sugar, oil of
turpentine, and other harmful materials. It seems
they did not understand these substances would
irritate the mucus membranes of the colon.

One medical doctor, H. Kellogg, in his book
Colon Hygiene, recommended sour milk enemas in
cases of colitis, chronic constipation, diarrhea,
excessive gas, chronic appendicitis, and chronic

diarrhea. In Kellogg's testing of five hundred people, he discovered that only fifteen percent had good bacteria in their colons. Why such a low count? Because we destroy good bacteria by eating too much sugar, caffeine, alcohol, meat and taking medications such as antibiotics!

Testimonial From One With PMS

Two weeks before my period, I would get irritable, with radical mood swings. I had pain and itching in the lower bowel area. Bloating caused weight gain and disoriented me.

I had an upper and lower GI and was given medications for my spastic colon condition. I was also treated for pre-menstrual syndrome. For three weeks now, I have had internal cleansing, and I altered my diet.

I had no pain before or during this menstrual period. I did not experience the bloating, disorientation, or mood swings.

This is miraculous!

Susan

Body Toxins

Authorities in the health field agree: toxins and poisons in the body stem from a toxic bowel. Remember, just because you have not taken social drugs or medications does not mean your body is not toxic.

When someone asks, "How do I know I have a toxic condition? I am healthy as a horse," I reply a typical Western diet consisting of too much meat, dairy, processed food, and sugar guarantees a certain amount of toxicity.

Sooner or later, the price for violating your body must be paid. Maybe not while you are young, but the time will come.

I guarantee it.

Cleansing the body eliminates blockages, dead cells, toxins, poisons, excess mucus, environmental pollutants, and greatly improves circulation. Our bodies are now the hazardous waste dumps when you realize the fact that **the average American**

26

consumes one pound of food additives per year! "Monosodium glutamate, sugar substitutes, dyes, preservatives (including nitrates), emulsifiers, fillers, waxes, tenderizers, texturizers, antifreezes, hormones and antibiotics are just a few of the chemicals added to a wide variety of processed foods. Tens of thousands of people have had adverse reactions, including death, to certain food chemical preservatives. Over 3000 chemical food additives hide in our food." (Quote from Vegetarian Times, August, 1995).

The Atlanta based Center for Disease Control and Prevention (CDC) estimates that Americans suffer at least 325,000 cases annually of food borne illnesses from fish. If you eat a shucked oyster, you're eating its intestines in a raw form. One study reviewed by the CDC by Doug Archer, Ph.D., shows that fin fish are less likely to cause food borne disease than other fish and beef or poultry, although shellfish is far more dangerous than either. (Isn't that an interesting scientific fact? In the Bible, God commanded His people to eat only the fish with fins and scales.)

Producers of the Prime Time Live ABC TV program recently enlisted "Longo" (whoever that is) to play the part of a typical consumer, sending her off to buy about 50 pounds of fish from markets in New York, Boston, Chicago and Baltimore. Then, the fish were tested in the laboratories for contamination. Twenty percent had harmful bacterial levels - higher than would be safe for humans to eat. About forty percent of them contained human fecal matter at a higher level than anyone should consume.

An EA study published in 1992 found DDE, a chemical resulting from the breakdown of the pesticide DDT, in more than 98% of 388 mostly freshwater sites. DDT was banned 22 years ago, yet it is still appearing on plates of seafood! Several other hazardous chemicals, PCBs and mercury, for example, turned up in more than 90% of the site samples.

27

The following information on toxins comes from exerpts of an article entitled, *"Hidden Dangers in Your Food and Water."* in the August, 1995, issue of *McCall's Magazine.*

Cell biologist Ana Soto, M.D., was perplexed. The breast-cancer cells she was working with in the laboratory were supposed to thrive only when 'fed' the female hormone estrogen. But the cells were growing without added estrogen. After months of puzzlement, Soto found the cancer cells' secret hormone source. The plastic equipment used in her experiment, it seemed, was releasing an estrogen-like chemical into the cell culture, causing the cancer cells to grow.

Our environment contains many man-made chemicals that may alter the effects of natural estrogen when they enter the human body in food and water, explains Terri Damstra, a toxicologist.

Here are some of the chemicals that may mimic or block estrogen in the body:

DDT and its breakdown product, DDE: *DDT is now banned in the United States, but is still present in our environment.*

Polychlorinated Biphenyls (PCBs): *These industrial compounds have been restricted in the United States but will linger in our environment for decades to come.*

Dioxins: *These chemical compounds - often produced during garbage incineration or as a result of paper bleaching - can be released into the air, water and soil.*

Experts point to the example of the now-infamous pregnancy drug diethylstilbestrol (DES). This drug, used between 1940 and 1971, was a powerful synthetic estrogen designed to prevent miscarriages. Its use resulted in a high rate of cancer and reproductive problems in both the women who took the drug and their offspring.

Women, having a greater percentage of body fat than men, can accumulate a heavy burden of these toxins, especially in fatty tissues such as the breasts. Laboratory studies at NIEHS show that inside the body, environmental estrogens can bind to estrogen receptors on a cell's surface and either mimic or block the effects of natural estrogen. 'We have to be careful about how we interpret these studies,' says Sandra Eirey of the Chemical Manufacturers Association (CMA). Several studies found that women with breast cancer tended to have higher concentrations of the organochlorines DDT, DDE or PCBs in their fat tissue than did other women.

Some evidence suggests that estrogenic and antiestrogenic pollutants can endanger developing fetuses. Other experts suspect that fetal exposure to dioxins may be responsible for a significant drop in sperm counts since 1940, which has been documented in the U.S. and in many other countries. In a single meal, a person may get PCBs in the fish and pesticides on the vegetables.

I believe there is an urgency to cleanse our bodies now in this polluted environment we are living in! Internal cleansing is the # 1 solution to ridding our bodies of the buildup of these toxic chemicals.

Hormone Additives

Much of our food contains hormones. Have you ever seen a man with breasts? Because he has eaten so much meat, those hormones respond to his body.

Most recently, hormones are being added to milk cows. Inevitably, if you do not get hormones in meat, you will get them in milk.

This is not natural.

Dairy Products

Some of my clients absolutely have to drink milk or consume dairy products. In these cases, science dictates that they drink raw milk or eat raw butter or raw cottage cheese. Today, these products are carefully certified by the dairies. Raw milk has been consumed for thousands of years. The body can break raw elements down and assimilate the natural nutrients far more effectively than it can homogenized, pasteurized, and fortified milk. Pasteurization kills the natural bacteria which help the body digest these products. I question the nutritional benefits of such refined foods. The French do not use pasteurization, and they have very few problems with colon cancer or heart disease, despite a daily diet of dairy products.

Remember, meat, processed food, sugars, and milk are mucus-forming. Undoubtedly, bacteria thrive on excess mucus.

Pneumonia Gone

Dear Millan:

My ten-year-old son was diagnosed with bronchial pneumonia. The doctors insisted he be hospitalized immediately.

Since I have not benefited from the medical system in the past, I refused and decided to have him receive ten sessions from you along with your cleansing program. After the fourth treatment, all symptoms of his pneumonia were gone.

He is eating healthy foods now and feels great. Thank you for being so gentle and loving towards my son.

Anonymous

Lactobacillus Bifidus

Did you know the intestines of an infant are free from putrefactive bacteria?

At the beginning of his research, Professor Tessier of Paris studied bad bacterial invasion of the intestines of young infants. He found that intestines of recently-born infants are swarming with putrefactive bacteria. Within a few days, however, the putrefactive bacteria disappeared. Of course, these were breast fed babies. He states:

Taking their place were particularly-shaped acid-forming microbes: Lactobacillus Bifidus. As long as Lactobacillus Bifidus

30

continues to multiply in the intestines of the child, the child enjoys good health. Significantly, the stools of that infant have no offensive odor, only a slight sourness.

As the child begins to eat table food - meat, pasteurized, homogenized milk, processed foods, and sugars - the child's stool begins to have a putrid odor. The putrefactive bacteria multiplies, and the lactobacillus bifidus, which came from the mother's milk, diminishes.

Then the child's sickly journey begins: colds, runny noses, ear infections, fever, and so forth.

Foul-smelling fecal matter is an indication of putrefactive bacteria. Decay is taking place right inside our wonderful bodies. Clients with this symptom can be sure they do not have the friendly bacterium lactobacillus bifidus which can be replenished in the system either orally or through solutions introduced by an implant after internal cleansing.

IT IS THAT SIMPLE.

Putrefactive Bacteria

With the right balance of favorable bacteria and coliform bacteria, bowel movements should have no odor.

I am sure you have heard you should cut down on meat...that meat is bad for you.

I tell my clients it is mucus-forming and has no fiber. Bacteria thrive on mucus. Because meat has no fiber, it can lodge in the colon and rot.

Putrefactive bacteria absorb into the body. The minute an animal is killed, putrefaction multiplies in the flesh. Even though you may cook this flesh, not all the bad bacteria are destroyed.

The flesh eaten, putrefactive bacteria get absorbed into the bloodstream. The bacteria eventually destroy the liver, kidneys, and other body-cleansing organs.

This finally leads to serious disease.

Autointoxication

Basically, we poison our bodies with our forks by eating the wrong foods and overeating. Remember, our bodies were never designed to handle flesh food.

Why do we bathe every day, brush our teeth, gargle with mouthwash, and pour on the perfume? We are trying to camouflage the smell of sewage inside our bodies.

This is chronic autointoxication.

This condition factors into most chronic disorders. Millions of putrefactive bacteria fill the flesh of dead animals.

I am proud of my twelve-year-old granddaughter Lareesa. She has not eaten any kind of flesh food since she was eight years old.

She says, "Grammy, I just love animals too much to eat them."

Rotting Meat

Sometime, take a piece of meat, any kind, and put it on your kitchen counter. Leave it there for a few days and see what happens. The stench will become unbearable.

Remember, if you were to eat that meat, it would likewise sit in your colon for days - sometimes even years - doing its job of rotting and stinking in your body.

Have you ever smelled someone's bad breath and caught the odor of feces? Do not think that because meat is properly refrigerated, the bad bacteria problem is resolved. Your warm body temperature creates a great atmosphere for destructive bacteria which is in the flesh food.

Medical experts worldwide recognize the extensive degeneration of the body's absorption of putrefactive bacteria in the intestinal tract. Constipation, diarrhea, headaches, and other illnesses result from this problem.

Being symptom-free does not equal being toxin-free.

Seniors

How unfortunate to hear a child say, "I don't want to sit next to Grandma; she smells."

Grandmas should be snuggled up to and cuddled with. That is one of the reasons God gave them to us.

One sign of putrefactive bacteria is a foul odor when defecating. The smell is offensive, requiring copious amounts of air freshener to mask the stench. One unfortunate senior lady told me she had to leave her mobile home every time her husband had a bowel movement.

Public Bathrooms

Have you ever gone into a public bathroom and could barely stand it; you wished you had a gas mask or something? It smelled like something crawled in there and died?

Well, guess what? Something is dead inside. But the decaying matter is not in the bathroom, it is in the colon! Who knows how long it has been there!

By now you may understand what I am suggesting. Perhaps you are disgusted by this topic. But I feel it needs to come out in the open (no pun intended).

Vegetarians

A significant difference between a flesh-food diet and a vegetarian diet is that the latter is non-putrefying. However, clients have come to me saying they are vegetarians and yet have numerous problems.

Upon questioning them further, I discover they drink tons of milk and consume a lot of fatty foods: cheese, donuts, candy, french fries, sodas, and who knows what else. But "they are vegetarians and proud of it." This does not make sense.

They might as well be septic tanks.

Those eating strictly vegetables, fruits, grains, legumes, raw nuts, and seeds have a diet that is non-putrefying. Fermentation takes place and forms harmless acids which aid in proper bowel elimination. Typically, stools will have a slightly sour, non-offensive odor.

A Convert's Story

My name is Myrna. I have been overweight and constipated since childhood.

When I was a teenager I grew to two hundred pounds. I started taking amphetamines and other drugs for almost fifteen years to lose weight and keep it off. I then started suffering skin problems. Brown patches covered my body.

I found out about fasting, internal cleansing, and became a vegetarian.

With the combination of diet and internal cleansing, my skin cleared. I also suffered allergies, and because of the cleansing they are gone.

Toxic Waste

Toxins are eliminated by the stomach, the blood, the gall bladder, the small intestine, and other organs. The poisons combine with undigested food passing through the body and into the large intestine.

The colon is the toxic dumping-ground of the body. If pockets of the colon are impacted with excess sewage - stagnating for God knows how long - how can proper elimination take place? The body then autointoxicates.

This becomes a vicious cycle.

The body reabsorbs putrefying bacteria and cannot expel it. Have you ever smelled someone's dirty hair or stinky feet?

Invariably, these poor folks have a putrid BM bound up in their large intestine. They are definitely not like the newborn babies of Professor Tessier's study which I previously mentioned.

Their stools likely result from a mixed diet of flesh foods, processed foods, sugar, and dairy products and weigh about five ounces. In contrast, stools from the diet consisting of vegetables, fruits, grains, legumes, raw nuts, and seeds are double in weight.

By the way, the healthy foods I have listed in this book are all fibrous foods which absorb calories. A high-fiber, natural diet is like a broom sweeping your body clean.

There are more than one hundred and fifty different species of bacteria which have been found in fecal matter. Of these species, more than a third posses pathogenic elements.

Soothing Water

Today, colon hydrotherapists know filtered, sterilized water at body temperature is best for administration of internal cleansing. It does not irritate the colon; therefore, it is not harmful. The client hardly feels the water going in, and with a knowledgeable, professional colon hydrotherapist, the cleansing is a comfortable procedure.

Ongoing Debate

Medical practitioners seem to be either whole-heartedly in favor of or adamantly against modern internal cleansing - there seem to be no intermediate opinions about it.

Those in favor are usually those who have benefited from it or have been open-minded. Condemners are nearly always those who have no such knowledge or experience.

I heard a pastor once say, "Prejudice is when you are down on something you are not up on."

Tracking the Progress of Internal Cleansing Through the Medical Literature

During the 1930's colon irrigation was regularly reviewed in the *New England Journal of Medicine, The British Medical Journal,* and *Lancet.* A comprehensive work was compiled by W. Kerr Russell, MD, assistant editor of the *British Journal of Physical Medicine* in 1932.

Several books published since 1981 by gastroenterologists refer to "the end of the colonic era" around 1960. Since 1960, ignorance, misinformation, and failure by the AMA to recognize internal cleansing's legitimacy have prevented standard medical doctors from prescribing the procedure. Consequently, within the medical establishment, prejudices surround the subject.

There is an unwillingness to examine the actual results of internal cleansing.

Throughout the 1980's, many bowel-related books were written. Their medical authors describe various bowel diseases, possible causes, and corrective surgical procedures. Some of these recent books approach better bowel health through diet. Some even mention enemas and colema boards.

Unfortunately, many discourage colon hydrotherapy - if they mention it at all - on purely unfounded facts. So many of them have not researched the subject, interviewed practitioners or patients involved in internal cleansing, or received treatment themselves.

In United States history, millions of people have had colon hydrotherapy. No complaints, illnesses, infections, or deaths have been reported as resulting from the procedure.

Legitimate criticisms of techniques and lack of sanitation while giving enemas can be found, but since the 1930's there has been no published scientific literature disclaiming the effectiveness of colon hydrotherapy.

An article in *The Journal of Joint and Manipulative Therapy* once mistakenly criticized colon hydrotherapy and enemas for removing all the bacteria from the lower GI tract. These critics seemed ignorant of the fact that most colon hydrotherapy is directed at removing poisons and restoring normal colon function.

So, as an adjunct to treatment, colon hydrotherapists implant lactobacillus acidophilus and bifidus cultures at the end of each session. This restores and promotes the recolonization of G.I. flora. Evidently, those authors neglected to investigate their allegations with proper studies.

What little criticism there is, therefore, does not attempt to examine the physiology, anatomy, microbiology, or pathology of the body in relation to effects of internal cleansing. Nor does it take into consideration current practices nationwide.

A study funded by the National College of Naturopathic Medicine was made to determine the effects of internal cleansing on serum electrolytes. Seventeen volunteers were recruited and colon hydrotherapy was administered. Serum electrolytes were measured by a single reference laboratory using an automated multichannel instrument prior to the first treatment and immediately before and after the third treatment. Serum electrolyte values were evaluated by a one-way analysis of variance for comparisons. None of these patients experienced signs or symptoms of water or electrolyte imbalance. While statistically significant, neither the means nor the individual serum levels dropped to values which would be considered clinically significant.

Inclusive Approach to Health

Not too long ago, doctors sneered at the thought of healing herbs. Yet progress is being made in the established medical profession, and change is being implemented in medical philosophy and attitudes, toward a more inclusive approach to health.

As recently as the early 1980's, official word linked heart disease to bad diet. Before that, the medical profession scoffed at the idea diet could affect the condition of the heart. Anyone who claimed otherwise was a quack, a far-out, fringe crackpot, a charlatan.

Doctor Proved Wrong

I had diabetes for seventeen years. My kidneys were not functioning correctly. Protein leaked into my urine instead of needy areas of my body. As a result, my tissues swelled with fluid. I gained twenty pounds. I swelled up so dangerously I was admitted to the hospital. There, the doctors had me taking sixteen of the strongest type of water pills a day.

While taking these pills, I saw spots, white dots, became dizzy and had a fast heartbeat. My doctor told me in five years I would be dead from kidney failure. I felt so bad I believed him. He asked if I had problems seeing. If so, he said, my eyes had developed lesions. When your kidneys go, your eyesight also goes.

I got worse because I was frightened, and I believed what he was saying. Then I got angry. I said to him, "Only God will determine my death, not you, doctor!"

Over a period of a few months, my determination to beat this thing changed. I prayed a lot, changed my eating habits, started exercising, moved to a new home, and started an internal cleansing program.

I was going through a detoxification stage. I developed cold-like symptoms.

My BUN (a test of kidney function) was seventy-five when I was ill and in the hospital. After the cleansing program, it went down to nineteen. The optimum level is seventeen.

I remember my doctor had told me I would never improve, and it was a matter of time for my kidneys to totally fail! If he could only see me now!

Sally

Potent Herbs

We need to remember that herbs form the basis of numerous refined pharmaceutical drugs. Some doctors marvel at the potency of herbs, and compare their few negative side effects to the processed and refined drugs prescribed which often have many side effects. There was a time when orthodox medicine dismissed past discoveries like vitamin C, the benefits of doing aerobic exercise, and a high fiber diet. In addition, the contributions of Omega 3 fish oil and beta carotene to combating cancer were scoffed at.

FDA Opposition

Health-food stores are doing their best business ever! More people recognize the benefits of organic vegetables, fruits, and over-the-counter herbs.

For years, the Food and Drug Administration (FDA) has kept a watchful eye on the sale of herbs and vitamins. At the writing of this book, an FDA bill now before congress would prohibit vitamin purchases without a doctor's prescription.

The FDA claims vitamins and herbs must be regulated to ensure public safety! FDA opponents believe regulation is just another way for those in the medical field to maintain control of the vitamin industry and its profits.

In 1992, a bill known as AB 856 worked its way to California's state senate. Originally, the proponents of this bill wanted to make both colon hydrotherapy and enemas illegal. But nurses "raised such a stink" (no pun intended) about the illegality of enemas, that the California Medical Association backed down.

The CMA changed the wording to apply only to colon hydrotherapy. They changed the bill midstream, wherein enemas would be permissible if prescribed by a doctor or administered in private homes by family members. The CMA's argument was that colon hydrotherapy is dangerous and should be banned. The weakness in this position was the lack of research or practical data to substantiate the claim.

Many observers believe the AMA is attempting to control alternative forms of treatment. More and more, patients are gravitating to workable methods keeping them healthy, and not just treating symptoms.

AB 856 is a reflection of the growing tension between the standard medical establishment and the lesser-known but potent "fringe" movement of wholistic professionals who provide products and services at considerably reduced costs. Worse, for standard medicine, patients have stated these remedies actually provide relief from many otherwise chronic or incurable ailments and diseases.

For these reasons, the proponents of colon hydrotherapy have advocated controlled research studies initiated by the medical establishment, but to no avail. These new studies would help convince the medical community that colon hydrotherapy is safe and effective. They would also bring colon hydrotherapy into the mainstream of modern medicine and bring it in front of the public. Research would also vindicate the many patients who, over the decades, have benefited physically, medically and psychologically from internal cleansing.

Harrassment of a Colon Hydrotherapist

The following account is from a letter written to me by a Colon Hydrotherapist living in San Francisco who was arrested for simply performing colon hydrotherapy.

In the Spring of 1991, I received a letter from the District Attorney's office requesting I make an appointment to come into his office. I honored his request and was accompanied by my attorney. I was informed that section 2052 of the Business and Professional Code prohibited me from performing colon hydrotherapy. My attorney informed him that this covered licensed professionals: including physicians, etc., who had either injured or killed their patients, and did not apply to me, since I had not killed or injured anyone. From that meeting on, my life was never the same. A process of dehumanization and personal violations ensued.

In February of 1992, an undercover person who identified herself as Janine Flannery called to make an appointment for colon hydrotherapy. She came to my office the following week. She filled out my intake sheet and took the procedure as far as putting on the gown I offered her. At this point, she just stalled by talking and asking questions like, 'What was this going to do to her?' and 'How does this equipment work?' She made me nervous! I suggested some books to read to give her additional information in helping her decide if this was in fact what she really wanted to do. We had spent the better part of 45 minutes at this point. Although she didn't follow through on the actual colon hydrotherapy, she paid me as though she had taken the colonic, requesting a receipt for services rendered, and I in return supplied her with one, as well as two leaflets copied from a book which they later used in court to show intent to commit the violation and to make a case around it.

Upon her departure, a sense of fear enveloped me. Within 5 minutes, a persistent knocking and ringing of the doorbell ensued. I would not answer the door. I walked to the window and to my astonishment I watched her ride away with a man I recognized as the Senior Investigator of the AMA. Anxiety stricken, I was comfortable I had said nor done NOTHING incriminating! Later, I found out she was wired for sound.

April 1, 1992, a client walked into my office at 9 a.m. Three minutes later there was a knocking at my door. I didn't answer because I was expecting my client only. The knocking became a relentless banging which in turn greatly upset my client. I reluctantly opened the door, and was faced with an impeccably dressed couple - a male and a female. I was greeted with, 'Are you Delores Hepburn?' and I replied, 'Yes, I am.' The female flashed her badge and identified the two of them. She said, 'You are under arrest.' I asked for her warrant. She grabbed my wrist and pulled me through the door onto my porch. She said, 'Don't make trouble.' I asked to get a purse and coat and was denied. One of them closed my door, locking my client in and me out with no keys or money. I was asked to face the wall. Then they handcuffed my arms behind me. At this moment, I felt embarrassment for what my neighbors might wonder about me. Did she murder someone? I was directed to a waiting car 100 yards up the street. I walked in handcuffs with the officers behind me - my head down. I did not want to see a neighbor looking at me in this position.

When we arrived at the police station I was asked to give fingerprints and let them take my picture. I refused, as it is my constitutional right to do so. I am not a criminal - I had done nothing wrong. I simply administered colon hydrotherapy. I was threatened with stripping me of all my clothes and being thrown into 'the hole' if I did not submit to a full set of fingerprints. When the officers in the station were angry enough, one of them twisted my arm up behind my back and cuffed me again. At this point, they put ink on my fingers and pressed paper to them. I was taken to a day room where I was further intimidated by drug addicts, prostitutes and other people displaying bruises on their faces inflicted by the police (according to them). I didn't speak the language of anyone in there. I felt sheer terror! I was told by a day officer, 'People in jail have no rights except to be fed and have a place to sleep.' At this time, I was informed that I would have to sleep on the floor without a blanket or a mat. The thought of sleeping on concrete and the fact that I had a foster child coming home from camp the next day quickly prompted me to do what I had to do to leave that awful place.

I let them take my picture and gave them a complete set of fingerprints. I signed my name under duress and walked away a free person as long as I showed up for court the next day. However, I still didn't have a coat nor did I have a quarter to make a phone call. I walked from the police station to the Salvation Army; from there I made a call to a friend who came to pick me up. As I waited, I reflected on what had happened to me. I felt raped multiple

42

times. Stripped of all my dignity and any self worth I ever had. Helpless and homeless because a locksmith was not going to get me into my house for free.

Now, I had the task of searching for the right attorney. I found it next to impossible to find an attorney to take my case and not sell me to the system. I finally decided that no-one could plead my case better than me! And so I did, with the help of a Pro Se Litigant. He was wonderful. The court was not always kind to me because I was my own representative. After every hearing, the District Attorney badgered me with 'You can't win your case. Give up and take the alternative program.' In essence, their proposal of an alternative program was an admission of guilt further penalized by community service projects. Also, during this time the California Medical Association was diligently attempting to get AB 856 passed to make colon hydrotherapy illegal. Where was the law I had broken? On June 12, 1992, my case was dismissed, bringing to a close 21 months and 11 days of emotional hell! If I was subjected to this kind of treatment without there being a law against the subject matter, what would happen if there was one? I am not a criminal, and have never broken any laws. I don't know what the future holds for me. Three years have gone by. I did not escape damage. My heart beats rapidly whenever someone knocks on my door, or a stranger parks near my home.

My enthusiasm and warmth I was once able to impart to each person I met is suppressed. Everyone who calls me is suspect. I am no longer comfortable to be my naturally energetic, animated self. I love working with people and helping them to become healthy. There is strength in numbers. Hopefully, in the future there will be many voices speaking out collectively to defend our right to continue this work. I am grateful to have had the

43

opportunity to grow by way of standing up for something I believe in.

Delores Hepburn

If you will take note, the case of Delores Hepburn was dismissed on June 12, 1992. That was right around the date the AB856 law banning colon hydrotherapy did not pass. This means there was no grounds to prosecute this colon hydrotherapist. I believe they were going to use her as an example to stop colon hydrotherapists from doing this therapy, but this bill did not pass, and their plans failed.

Allergy Relief

I could not believe allergy tests revealed I had forty allergies!

That was two years ago. Last year I undertook a series of doctor-recommended shots. Still, I continued to feel half-dead, weak, sick, and had no energy.

I had constant colds: a runny nose and sore throat. When I began internal cleansing, lots of stringy old feces and ropy stuff came out.

I followed my colon hydrotherapist's detoxification program to the "T." I have since lost ten pounds - a pleasant surprise - and people at work have commented on how good I look. They say that my eyes are brighter and my skin looks better.

Last night I saw an old beau who had not shown much interest in me previously. He appeared very interested, attentive, and commented on how well I looked!

Yesterday I went back to my doctor. He did the allergy tests again and discovered only two allergies!

He said, "Whatever you're doing, keep doing it, because it's working!"

I must say the whole colon cleansing program has been beneficial. For once, my bowel movements are regular and elimination is easier.

I am happier and life, overall, is more balanced. I have always been a compulsive eater, and finally my appetite is more in control thanks to the cleansing. It is such an exhilarating feeling to have good health and energy.

Christy R.

Present History

Internal cleansing has been used for centuries; however, only in present history has it become one of the most silenced topics of discussion among the lay public and its doctors. It is ironic this is the case now, when internal cleansing is needed most - the most toxic time in our history.

Year-long Illness Disappears

Dear Millan:

I want to thank you and Judy for being your competent, professional and caring selves. Your treatments were very effective, and we believe I have now become completely cured of my epilepsy condition that has plagued me over the past year. My system feels much different and I feel healthier than I have in a long time. Your program was vital for complete success. Thank you and Judy for being there. Here's wishing you the very best in life.

Love,
Dave G.

CHAPTER TWO

WHAT COLON HYDROTHERAPY IS: COLON HYDROTHERAPY VS. ENEMAS

The Enema

Chances are, you have heard of, and maybe even had, an enema. But few people have heard of colon hydrotherapy.

If you have had an enema, you may recall discomfort. It may have been inconvenient. Moreover, if you were unlucky, you could not hold water in long enough, and you surrendered to the need to stool. When you did sit on the toilet, the results were probably not satisfactory. You may have received nowhere near the relief you were seeking.

The reason for this is the basic nature of an enema: a rush of water is introduced into the rectum, more or less uncomfortably, under unsafe pressure. This, it is hoped, will both stimulate the rectal evacuation reflex and somewhat soften hardened feces, allowing them to pass into the toilet at the end of the specified time.

As medical remedies go, enemas are naturally primitive and crude. The "equipment" consists of a bag (or squeeze bulb) to hold water (or another solution - soap, detergent, and turpentine solutions have even been used, to ill effect!), and a rectal insertion hose or tube to deliver the liquid - one way only.

There was a time three-foot tubes were inserted into the colon!

Coupling the physics of water and gravity with the construction of the colon, an enema can only have a very limited effect. Its water usually reaches just past the sigmoid, which is next to the rectum.

The enema solution hardly reaches the colon opening, because once the bag empties, pressure forcing water in stops. The water only marginally

47

softens stools accumulated in the lower area. Remember, the colon is 5 to 5 1/2 feet long!

If stools are really impacted, water barely helps. Holding it in can be excruciatingly uncomfortable. The rectum's natural reflex is to immediately release liquid, as in diarrhea.

What an enema does is simulate diarrhea.

If you have ever had diarrhea, you know the screaming urgency to evacuate that water immediately. Desperation characterizes someone receiving an enema for constipation relief. Uninstructed individuals who give themselves enemas have to get to their feet from a prone position on the floor - without control of their overloaded bowels.

When you are finally allowed to make your way gingerly to the toilet (on the other side of the galaxy, it seems!), water gushes out in a great splashing rush, hardly changed from when it went in.

You break out anew in alternating waves of hot flashes and cold sweats. The greatest urge in memory to defecate overwhelms you, and you push and strain.

There is gas and more water.

Between anal spasms, you may or may not be successful. You concentrate and pray for it to be over.

If you are successful, you stagger away - thankful it is over.

In my home cleansing program, the booklet includes easy instructions on how to do an enema comfortably, correctly and effectively to achieve the best results.

An Enema User's Account

I used to be very ill: I had arthritis and migraine headaches. I was in and out of hospitals. I thought vitamins were only taken to stay well. Before I knew about internal cleansing, I used to do four enemas a day.

I was disgusted and discouraged.

I came home one day and decided to throw every unhealthy food out of my cupboards. I never drink coffee, tea, coke, or Pepsi anymore.

When I changed my diet and did the complete cleansing program, the arthritis and the migraine headaches went away.

Angelina

Enemas Can be Harmful

An enema operates by gravity. To empty water into the rectum, the bag's height can vary from a couple of inches to as much as eight feet.

The water pressure per square inch into the rectum and coursing against its delicate membranes can be unsafe without proper instruction. At 4 1/2 feet high, an enema averages two pounds or more per square inch.

That more damage is not done is a compliment to nurses and orderlies administering enemas before surgeries, irradiating the lower G.I. tract with barium for X-rays, or working in medical offices to alleviate desperate clients' constipation.

Records contain cases of damage caused by incorrect administration of enemas. There are no such records for modern colon hydrotherapy.

A Better Way: Colon Hydrotherapy

A better way is a complete internal cleansing program.

It is gentle, painless, and odorless. It is clean and dry. It is even relaxing, and, what is more, you learn nutritional information from your colon hydrotherapist during the procedure. It is comfortable - you can lie down and take a break.

It is not humiliating - you will not fail.

It is not embarrassing; my clients are totally covered. It is not undignified.

There is no discomfort. It is not stressful. My clients even receive an abdominal massage!

Afterwards, my clients feel vibrant and are on their way to better health.

In contrast to the minimal standards required for enemas, colon hydrotherapy's standards are high. We use state-of-the-art, name-brand equipment mounted next to the table on which the client lies during the procedure. This internal cleansing equipment is capable of controlling water pressure, temperature, and flow.

The equipment features a clear glass, florescent-lighted view tube. Through this, any discharge is observed and examined. The tube is also a direct disposal line for toxins and stool.

Relaxing and Gentle

There is no discomfort, no offensive odors, and no mess. The client does nothing; the equipment does all the work.

At my office, clients provide their health history and discuss with me their health needs, concerns, and the general state of their current health. I have treated children as young as eight years old, and those as old as ninety-four years.

The colon hydrotherapist puts the client at ease by attending to questions, explaining functions of the equipment, and, using the charts on the wall, describing how the procedure is done. I reassure my client of my gentleness.

The Actual Therapy

When a client arrives at the colon hydrotherapist's office, he or she is escorted into the bathroom and given a hospital gown. The client removes all clothes from the waist down, except socks.

The client at this time empties the bladder completely. When the client emerges (modestly clutching the gaping gown closed in back!), client and therapist go into the internal cleansing room.

The client climbs up onto the comfortably padded table (which resembles a doctor's examining table), adjacent to the ultra-modern internal cleansing equipment.

It is imperative that the colon hydrotherapist is working with modern, name-brand equipment, outfitted with safety features, sanitation with ultraviolet light, and geared to use various implements and administer oxygen.

Many health practitioners believe that more oxygen can be absorbed through the colon than through the lungs. This oxygen gets absorbed into the bloodstream and bathes the cells in the body.

If there is no name brand on the equipment, the client should run, not walk, out of that office. And, of course, the colon hydrotherapist must be professional, certified, and knowledgeable.

She (most colon hydrotherapists are women) must monitor the progress of the internal cleansing, massage the client's colon through the abdomen, and satisfactorily explain the procedure of cleansing the colon. Lymphatic massage during the therapy can be administered as well, for excellent release of toxins and poisons. She should explain what she is doing and what is happening in the digestive tract.

Just before administering the colon hydrotherapy, the ileocecal valve must be correctly closed by the therapist. This is to prevent any fecal matter or toxins in the colon from "engrossing" or being back flushed (allowed back into the small intestine).

Once the ileocecal valve is securely closed, the client lies on the right side, drawing knees to chest in the fetal position. By this time, the client feels comfortable with the therapist.

It is very important that the colon hydrotherapist not only be knowledgeable but also be gentle and caring. The client can assist in inserting the speculum.

The insertion should be completely painless.

When the speculum is in place, the colon hydrotherapist helps the client roll over onto the back. Again, knees are bent, but feet are flat on the table.

The client's hospital gown ensures complete coverage.

When the client is comfortable and everything is in place, the process begins.

The disposable speculum is only one inch in diameter and rests comfortably in the rectal area. The speculum not only delivers water into the colon, it also removes it, as two separate hoses are attached to the other end of the speculum. One hose admits sanitized water and the other allows expulsion of feces.

The colon hydrotherapist turns on the water gradually. The water temperature is the same as the body temperature. Most people do not even notice the water because of this, and so agree that this is a smooth and comfortable procedure. The colon hydrotherapist will pulsate the output tube as she administers the internal cleansing. The client may not even feel this, since it is comfortable. The purpose of the pulsation is to loosen fecal matter in the lower end of the bowel by simulating peristaltic waves. Pulsating the output tube also helps by preventing too much water from getting behind and around the feces.

If the client has excess gas, it takes a little longer for the stool to eliminate. The water cannot get past the gas and travel further up the colon.

At each session, both client and colon hydrotherapist will observe dislodged feces floating through the view tube which is contained in the equipment.

Often during a session I cannot help exclaiming to clients, "Look at what you are eliminating!"

The two of us then closely examine the contents flowing through the well-lighted tube. We may notice blotchy brown clouds, flecks, and more solid matter of black, brown, or even yellow. Sometimes the discharge is ropy-looking or has ridges. I have even seen hair and vitamins tumbling down the view tube during a session.

We see old matter, new matter, and sometimes no matter at all.

Sometimes it is necessary for the client to sit on the toilet to expel (this is very rare, as the equipment is most often capable of doing the job).

Muscle tone of the colon is judged by the vigor of expulsion and the vibration of the observation tube as noted by the therapist. There could be slight cramping, similar to that of menstrual cramps (which can be helped through internal cleansing).

Gas Bubbles

Sometimes little bubbles furiously race by through the viewing tube of the equipment. This is excess gas. Isn't it nice this is a closed system? During many sessions clients note these gas bubbles. While it is natural to have a certain amount of gas, excess gas is not normal and is an indication of a toxic, impacted colon. Most excess gas is caused by excess feces in the colon, decomposing just like a carcass out in a field.

This offensive gas is the byproduct of putrefied bacteria. These organisms break down and re-digest previously digested waste material that should have been excreted long ago. Stress, excitement and anxiety can also cause excess gas.

Excess gas is a common experience of clients, and is something to be expected while on a cleansing program.

Certain foods like broccoli, cauliflower, onions, garlic, cabbage, and cucumbers can also cause gas. Or, foods eaten in wrong combination can produce flatulence. Another possible cause might be a lactobacillus and coliform bacteria imbalance.

For all these reasons, it is normal to have some gas while on a cleansing program. But a client should hang in there; it is only temporary. When this period is over, the stools will no longer have an offensive odor.

During a single colon cleansing session the client's colon hydrotherapist typically fills and evacuates the water four or more times. Many people benefit from at least ten treatments of about forty-five minutes each before achieving a state of health, vigor, youthfulness, and well-being.

An attractive young woman was correcting her eating habits, but still had bowel movements only once every seven days or so. During her first session, the water could not reach past the sigmoid, just above the rectum; her colon was that badly impacted.

That happens sometimes because of a lifetime of poor eating habits. A good diet alone cannot easily tone a flaccid, toxic colon.

I instructed her to sit on the toilet and eliminate. It took an extended series of cleansings, during which all the old impacted sewage was expelled. The results of the cleansing indicated that, she was doing just fine.

After a session of forty-five minutes to an hour, the water passing through the viewtube usually becomes bubblefree and clear.

Newcomers to the procedure are often nervous and sometimes apprehensive, as we all are of the unknown. But before long, they feel comfortable with the protocol and think nothing of it.

They are smiling and relaxed.

There is no pain, no personal anxiety, only soothing conversation and gentle massage, interesting viewing, and perceptible health benefits. Fear and tension vanish with the sewage down the drain.

When the procedure is finished, the client is again rolled into the fetal position on the left side, and the speculum is gently and slowly withdrawn.

Totally covered, the client is rolled again onto the back and helped to a sitting position. At this time, it is not uncommon to feel a little stiff from lying in the same position for an hour. Clients take this opportunity to limber up a little.

Next, the hydrotherapist helps the client down from the table to go into the bathroom, eliminate, and get back into street clothes. By this time, most people feel reinvigorated, light-footed, and full of bouncy energy.

Victory Over PMS

Think you have premenstrual syndrome? It could be, but some symptoms are very similar to a simply unhealthy colon crying out desperately for help, as in my client Cory's case:

Before: Her abdomen hurt, and she was very bloated. She suffered from chronic fatigue, and indigestion. Her hair was thin, skin was dry and breaking out, and her menstruation was irregular.

She was carrying twenty pounds of water weight.

Her thinking was fuzzy, and she had a hard time concentrating. Weak and short of breath; she only urinated one to two times a day.

Bowels: diarrhea and then constipation. She was not digesting food (whole pieces came out), could not sweat, and could not work or hold a job. In addition, she had goiters and candidasis.

After internal cleansing: Cory had tremendous energy. She enjoys swimming and roller-blading, and her digestion is good. Skin is clear and soft, and her hair is thicker than ever before in her whole life. Menstruation is back to normal, and her goiters are gone. Water weight is gone, as well as the candidiasis.

Her thought processes are great: she is in school and working. In fact, she started her own business.

As depressed as she was before, now she is very happy. Her bad breath is gone!

Chronic illness can be a thing of the past. When your body is clean, your immune system is raised and is better able to combat viral attacks from outside the body, rather than fighting toxins produced by the garbage rotting inside .

Discomfort and Cramping

I have asked many doctors what causes cramping during internal cleansing, and they all give different answers. I believe it is because the colon most likely has some narrow areas. It is the movement of the cleansing herbs and stool, expanding the colon walls through these passages, that causes discomfort.

A head pressure of one foot will cause water to reach the cecum in two to five minutes with professional equipment. This will not happen when I am treating someone with spastic colon or colitis.

When the cecum is chronically irritated, some health practitioners suspect the client to have conditions such as the following: arthritis, sinusitis, tonsillitis, or infection.

A toxic colon can overwork the liver, causing the liver to enlarge, and lead to a congested liver. This condition would be indicated by a colon displacement at the hepatic flexure as shown on an X-ray .

It is very important that a client not eat food two hours before the internal cleansing appointment, but may drink liquids such as juice, herb teas, and water. The client may eat afterwards.

I have had clients tell me that after their treatment they were ravenous, not for junk food but for a salad or other healthy meal.

It is so wonderful to know that internal cleansing can stop the vicious cycle of craving garbage food.

Hot water may be effective in eliminating various parasites. Studies have shown that temperatures of 104 to 110 degrees for five to fifteen minutes is sufficient to kill amoebas and other protozoans and parasites of the colon.

I have heard many therapists who insert hot water (body temperature, of course) and then reduce the temperature, claiming the cold water will cause peristalsis in the colon.

I do not believe this is good for the client and have found it really does not achieve promised results. Dr. Harvey Kellogg, in his book *Colon Hygiene,* states this practice can be very painful and should be discouraged.

Free From Medications!

For 5 years I have been in and out of doctors offices, complaining about sharp pains by my right side. The doctors put me on different prescribed medications. Nothing helped. They all told me it was irritable bowel syndrome, for which they said there is no cure. They said it was due to stress. I spent literally three to five thousand dollars in about four years on medications - all to no avail! Recently, my chiropractor suggested internal cleansing. Even after the first session I felt 80% better. I'm now on my 7th session, and have continued relief. My bowels now move more regularly without any of the pain I've experienced before. I highly recommend internal cleansing to everybody.

Signed,
Lisa

Properly-trained Colon Hydrotherapists

Clients must be very careful that their colon hydrotherapists are fully qualified, certified, and recommended by others. I cannot emphasize enough the importance of a properly trained, certified colon hydrotherapist.

One client told me she had gone to a so-called colon hydrotherapist to have therapy. First the therapist inserted the speculum. She then turned the client over on her back, and began to turn the water on. The client then asked her what she was doing: "Are you aware that this speculum is in my vagina?" The therapist described above was no bargain! Clients should seek colon hydrotherapists who demonstrate the utmost concern for the health and well-being of clients rather than bargaining-table proposals. A properly educated, certified colon hydrotherapist is imperative.

With professional equipment, colon hydrotherapists can get water all the way up to the cecum, which is why it is so important that the ileocecal valve be properly closed. At this point we are essentially water-massaging and cleansing the entire 5 1/2 foot long colon!

Lymphatic Massage

Roxanne Watson, my daughter, also a colon hydrotherapist, states:

When a client is given a lymphatic massage before internal cleansing, the lymphatic system releases a great amount of tiny mucus particles or a cloudy substance. This can be seen through the view tube.

Different substances always drain from the body after a pre-treatment of lymphatic massage.

My sauna clients dump a great deal of matter from the liver. They release incredible amounts of toxins for the full forty-five minutes. Clients have gone to other colon hydrotherapists, receiving as many as fifty sessions. Neither cleansing herbs nor any cleansing program was ever recommended with their sessions.

I put one woman, with fifty prior sessions, on a cleansing program, and in four sessions she dumped a large quantity of toxins the full forty-five minutes of each colonic. She said in all the other sessions combined she had not released so much as she had with my cleansing program.

Here is a person who had gone to a colon hydrotherapist with twelve years' experience yet who still did not put clients on any kind of cleansing program to help rid the body of toxins, poisons, and old fecal matter. How unfortunate to have a colon hydrotherapist who knows nothing about cleansing herbs or a good cleansing program!

Blocked Colons

Believe me, the colon builds up blockage just like our plumbing at home or our car's engine.

People have many pounds of feces in the colon! Autopsies I have witnessed confirm this to be true.

If you are driving your car and the red light on your dash indicates there is a problem, do you cover the light with tape and keep right on going as though the problem has been resolved?

Of course not.

Yet we do the same to our bodies when we feel a pain or ache. We go to the doctor's office and get a prescription to mask pain.

We seldom go further to get to the real cause and not just treat the symptoms. Our body parts are so interconnected, that, perhaps, when we hurt we could consider cleaning out the colon and detoxifying the system. The body could hurt because it is in a state of autointoxication.

Your body cannot assimilate nutrients if it is toxic. It is that simple.

We buy hundreds of vitamins and minerals and expect to feel better. Yet often we do not. Then we wonder why.

A client must clean out the body, then add the nutrition. See and feel the difference.

Some clients say, "Gee, what is wrong? Why don't I feel better?"

They change their diets and eat nutritious foods. They virtually cut out meat, dairy, and processed foods. They start exercise programs and take the best vitamins and minerals money can buy.

Yet why do they not feel better?

They must clean out their systems! There are many reasons we are unhealthy: a poor diet, a toxic system, lack of exercise, heredity, and environment.

Four Steps To Good Health

There are four steps to good health.

First, ultimately it would be good if humans could exclusively eat vegetables - fruits, grains, legumes, raw nuts and seeds, and very little fish, chicken, and turkey. I know this must seem like an impossible objective for most reading this book, but the closer one comes to it, the better one feels.

Second, cleanse the body.

Third, exercise, whether it be walking, aerobics, bike-riding, etc.

Fourth, because many nutrients are lacking in so many foods, a daily intake of good vitamins and minerals is essential.

Testimonial

I have received a series of ten internal cleansing sessions and did the detox program. I have suffered from migraine headaches and obesity in the past. Now the migraines have incredibly diminished and I have lost twenty pounds. My out-of-control eating is behind me now. Last week I saw a friend I had not seen in over a month, and she said "What have you been doing? Your face looks glowing, and I can tell you lost weight."

I did not want to tell her I've been getting internal cleansing, because I knew she wouldn't understand. She is not an open-minded person. I just told her, "I've changed my diet." I feel great now.

Valerie

A Natural Enema

When my clients get themselves into a bind (no pun intended) and cannot get to a colon hydrotherapist, the following recipe produces excellent results:

1/2 pint of molasses
1/2 pint warm, distilled water

Mix solution and use in an enema bag to flush out the colon.

This solution is harmless and very agreeable with the colon. Another way my clients evacuate their colons is to lie on their backs and gently knead their lower abdomens with their fists.

Abnormal Colons

It has been reported that in one case a thirty-eight-year-old man died, and when his colon was examined it was 19 inches in diameter and weighed almost one hundred pounds. In contrast, a normal colon is 2 to 2 1/2 inches in diameter.

Look around at many of the people with potbellies. Granted, fat is there, but also pocketed in the colon are pounds of old, impacted stool.

The danger is that when this impacted stool bursts through colon walls and becomes infected, diverticulitis results. This is a very common condition; moreover, it is evident that half of my clients suffer from hemorrhoids.

In his book, Dr. Norman Walker tells of a young epileptic patient of his. Walker recommended six weeks of internal cleansing for the girl. After the

60

fifth week, there were no visible results, and the patient's family was discouraged. Finally, after the end of the fifth week, lo and behold, this young lady passed a fist-full of worms during her session.

After that, she never had another epileptic seizure.

Years of abuse to our bodies cannot be remedied overnight. We live in a society of instant results, yet obtaining good health just does not work that way.

Women with prolapsed, transverse colons (from my research, seventy percent of people in the western world have prolapsed colons), are likely to have some female problems: positive Pap smears, vaginal infections, discharge, and so forth.

A normal-looking colon is very rare. Most X-rays show twisted, looped, and ballooned colons.

Why?

Because of diet.

We eat very little fiber foods and way too much of the wrong foods. One time, a nurse told me she watched a doctor perform colon surgery. The surgeon observed feces in the patient's colon and just sewed it back up, leaving the fecal matter right where it was.

Influences on Regularity

Pleasurable emotions and excitement that one may experience can positively affect the colon toward elimination. On the other hand, depression, despondency, anger, the desire for revenge, bitterness, and stress can halt the functioning of the digestive system and can cause constipation. Animal and human studies have proven this.

Exercise is very important in keeping the colon healthy. I know a person who jumps on the trampoline daily to move her bowels. And it works! She swears by it and recommends it to others.

When one sits a lot, the colon muscles do not function properly. Many clients are truck drivers or airplane pilots who sit for long periods and are not able to go to the bathroom when the urge hits them.

Posture has been mentioned time and again among health authorities and cannot be emphasized enough; it is vital to the proper functioning of the colon.

Be aware of how you are standing. Are your shoulders back? Is your chest out? Is your head up high?

How about when you are sitting? Are you straight up? Is your chin up? You will find correct posture aids greatly in bowel elimination.

CHAPTER THREE

CULTURAL AND SOCIETAL ATTITUDES
TOWARDS BODY ELIMINATION

Cultural Taboos

When was the last time you said to a friend or family member, "Did you have a good bowel movement today? Do you think it all came out?" Or, "You know, my bowels haven't moved for a few days lately." Or, "Boy, I sure have a lot of gas today, so look out!"

Even in their offices, many American doctors tend to avoid anything pertaining to the colon. Perhaps some find the subject offensive and below their dignity and training.

In the morning, if your boss comes into the office grumpy, could it be because his bowels did not move or completely eliminate?

Discussion relating to bowel movements should not be considered "offensive," yet this is the case in our culture. By contrast, all areas of sex are discussed openly, with no embarrassment. Sex was also an "unspeakable" only thirty years ago, considered unfit for polite conversation. It was a private, very personal and intimate subject. It was usually not even mentioned between a married man and woman, and certainly not to anyone else.

The recent sexual revolution is due largely to educational efforts, such as sex-education in classrooms, and wide exposure through the media. Not to be forgotten is the advent of the Pill, which changed practically overnight women's sexual behavior.

Open discussion of bowel habits, conditions, and contents is still a taboo subject in our culture.

Once, in a TV interview, when I started discussing bowel movement, the host of the program actually started squirming and making the funniest faces. It was pathetic. Boy, the station's phone sure rang off the hook after that show, all from people wanting more information about internal cleansing.

Past Cultures

There is some indication in past cultures this particular bodily function and its product were not considered offensive, or at least not compared to today. The putrid odor makes it currently offensive.

In ancient Japan, public contests were held to see who in a town could break wind loudest and longest. Winners were awarded many prizes and received great acclaim.

We have come a long way since then!

I am sure their gas was not offensive, because otherwise they certainly would not be public heroes; people would run the opposite direction. This shows in earlier days there was nothing disgusting or shameful about their lower digestive system.

During the Roman Empire, Romans not only had bath houses but also social toilets. These social toilets were lounge benches with holes in them. There men sat and visited while they defecated. This may indicate that their bowel movements did not have an offensive odor; certainly their normal diet was high in fiber-plant foods.

This photo of a "social toilet" was taken in a castle in Europe.

David Louis, in 2001 *Fascinating Facts*, states:
Undertakers report that human bodies do not deteriorate as quickly as they used to. The reason for this, they believe, is that the modern diet contains so many preservatives that these chemicals tend to prevent the body from decomposing too rapidly after.

Tell me we do not need to cleanse our bodies. It was told to me by a military doctor that during the Vietnamese war, the bodies of the American soldiers decomposed very slowly in comparison to the bodies of the Vietnamese soldiers.

A Simple Solution

Did you know bowel movements of breast-fed infants have no offensive odor? Adult stools should be that way, and can be, if we clean out our presently polluted colon and eat God-made foods.

People accept without question - yet equally without substantiation - that all that is medically possible is being done to find cures and other alleviating treatments for the diseases plaguing us daily. Supposedly, our best interest is the concern. All avenues are explored and clues followed on diseases' causes and ultimate destruction, so that all humankind - or at least, all Americans - can finally live disease free.

But this is not happening.

Colon research and its direct relationship to disease and health are not being pursued by the great institutions in our country.

The ultimate solution is simple and cheap; internal cleansing. As a society, we have become so enamored with expensive, complicated technologies that we do not trust humble procedures, dating back to ancient times, to possibly work today. The popular thinking seems to say, "If it is not expensive and spectacular, it cannot be any good."

Internal cleansing is too simple.

A Success Story

On April 25, I had my first internal cleansing session. I was constipated,

65

overweight, gassy, and for years took three types of anti-depressants. I was never able to get off them.

I received fourteen hydrotherapy treatments, and my diet improved. The results were great: more regular BM's, exercising, down to one anti-depressant, clear head, more energy, and I am happier.

Anonymous

Individual Difference

An instance comes to mind of a hospital administrator in her mid-forties. The woman heard about internal cleansing and decided to give it a try.

She had a lot of mild problems - stress, lack of energy - and was continually upset. Following my instructions to a "T," she had a series of sessions and observed the recommended diet and cleansing program.

After a few sessions, this woman started to eliminate a lot of old fecal matter, shed weight, and her energy level improved. Her disposition changed. She was more optimistic, a lot happier.

By the time she had completed her series, she was a changed woman. Interestingly enough, a month later her twenty-two-year-old daughter came in for a session (the two were living together).

The daughter said, "You know, when my mother first came to you, she was impossible to live with. She would argue, and she was crabby. She was miserable. Now she is more pleasant to be around; she is easy to get along with and is a joy. What a difference! She is another person."

The hospital administrator indicated to me her colleagues were telling her she looked wonderful. They wondered what was different about her. They could not pinpoint the difference, and she could not tell them she was cleansing the inside of her body.

Internal Cleansing:
An Inexpensive, Simple Procedure

An hour of internal cleansing at the current rate is quite reasonable, considering all one gets for the money. It is a simple, relaxing procedure where the recipient lies supinely and has a safe washing of the colon.

There is no expensive operating room or multiple trained staff; no needles, band-aids, scrubs, shaves, scalpels, or anesthesia; no cutting, sawing, breaking, clamping, stitching, or stapling; no time in a recovery room, no cold room temperature to bring your temperature and blood pressure down, and no prosthetics.

All potentially harmful toxins and sewage are gently cleansed out of the body's last-stop distribution point: the colon.

The result is surprisingly pleasant. Even after the first treatment, the client feels much better. It is like getting a bath inside your body.

There are no drugs or prescriptions to fill afterward that could possibly become addictive and certainly have side effects. No needles or bandaids, before, during, or after, anywhere for anything. No blood lost, transfused, or soiling skin and clothes. No yellow or purple stains from antiseptic washes and markings. No bruising, deep tissue damage, or nausea.

Healthy Octogenarian

One eighty-seven-year-old client sees me every ten days for her internal cleansing. After being treated by a clinic in Tijuana ten years ago for breast cancer, her cancer went into remission. She became a strict vegetarian and underwent colon cleansing. She does internal cleansing regularly for prevention.

Her mind is alert, and she remembers much of her past. This dear lady has a lot of energy! Once in a while, she forgets her appointment with me, but, all in all, she is remarkable.

Toilet Training Attitudes

Because of societal attitudes, it is doubtful the medical establishment will ever meaningfully research the benefits of internal cleansing.

The root of our reluctance to deal with human elimination and waste is psychological; it has a great deal to do with how we as a society teach our children how and when to eliminate.

Today the preferred term, reflecting this developmental reality, is "potty training;" what the child does is "toilet learning."

This is because until children are twenty to thirty-six months old, they do not have the completed nerve circuitry to control their sphincters or to connect urinating and bowel movements to being wet or soiled; they do not have the sensations of tightening or relaxing the muscles to pass or hold urine or feces.

Babies urinate or defecate, their bodies letting go as needed, as purely unconsciously as lungs breathing or hearts beating. It is cruel to force them to meet grownup expectations and standards.

During the Victorian era and the Age of Reason, bodily functions were considered to be necessary evils to the existence of the glorious human mind. They were banned from public notice, at least in the more refined upper strata of society.

Bodily functions were vulgar, common, mean, and unfit for discourse among educated and dignified people. Regimens were enforced, by dictates of betters, but were never mentioned. People ate on schedule, slept on schedule - everything was done according to schedule. People even eliminated on schedule.

Naturally, children were reared on a schedule.

Men, the only recognized medical authorities, dictated children must be disciplined and trained into civilized young men and ladies. These doctors prescribed a rigid schedule for everything: nursing, changing diapers, wraps, clothes, even crying and holding and loving.

Picking up a baby to hold, cuddle, and kiss was discouraged on the grounds it would make the child - especially a boy - a weakling, one who would grow up to be a spineless coward as an adult.

Babies were to begin "potty training" - like puppies - at six months, no later. Even today, some parents boast their children were "potty trained" at nine or ten months.

Natural biological development has set the stage for our present inability to accept our lower intestine's function and its vital importance. Many see human bodies as disgusting, vile, and even sinful because they die and decay.

Others fail to value research, public discourse, education, and attentive care of the colon as much as valuing lungs for breathing, hearts for circulation, blood for distributing oxygen and nutrients to every cell, genitals for sexual pleasure, and brains for intellect, mind, imagination, and soul.

Try as we might to avoid the subject, there is no getting around the fact that digestion includes elimination.

All other processes depend on correctly functioning, healthy kidneys and colon.

People die if they cannot eliminate urine or fecal matter. Inherited repulsion by body stool is paradoxical. It is a wonder people even defecate once a day instead of a minimum of three times daily as they really should. Healthy elimination is defecation after each meal. True, urine and feces present possible contamination with disease bacteria and other pathogens. Moreover, because of poor diet or medication in the system, urine and feces smell repulsive.

Good hygiene demands treating body waste in a prudent manner. Beyond that, urine and feces are not especially disgusting, particularly in a child's eyes.

At a few months old, children go through a normal phase of "discovering" their feces. One day, usually after a nap, an infant wriggles out of a thoroughly soaked, full diaper, and recognizes in its contents the perfect art medium!

The infant proceeds to decorate everything in reach, usually his crib and the nearest walls, with this marvelous dark paint. Along the way, the child might sample the mess as food, perhaps as chocolate, which it resembles smeared on hands and face.

When Mom opens the nursery door, Junior greets her in ecstatic glee and pride, eager to show off his latest masterpiece and share with her his expressive - and delicious! - paint-cum-dessert. Too bad Mom usually does not appreciate her offspring's budding artistic talent or gourmet tendencies!

Mom's reaction can indicate how she feels about her own body and its functions and how she will introduce her child to the toilet.

If Mom feels repulsed and embarrassed about defecation, she will "toilet train" her child, as she was "toilet-trained." She will closely watch her baby for signs he is having a bowel movement; maybe he scrunches up his face and stops what he is doing, or gives some sign.

At the first hint, she will whisk him to the bathroom, where she will plop him on his potty seat, maybe even strapping him in, giving him toys to play with or goodies to eat until he "goes." While she waits, her anxiety and perhaps impatience will be palpable to her little one. When he goes, she will quickly wipe him, often over her knee or the edge of the tub. He struggles to breathe while she holds him down, and she will make disgusted faces, maybe even hold her nose, as she hurriedly dumps the feces into the big toilet and flushes them down.

With a huge whooshing and sucking noise and a frighteningly furious swirl of savage waters, that little boy watches part of him - for these little pieces came out of him - be eaten and swallowed.

If after that trauma the little boy struggles to protect more pieces of himself by retaining his bowel movements, he becomes constipated. His mother increases her disgust and probably verbally abuses him, threatening dire punishment. She may coerce him, either by prolonged sessions on the potty or applying a home enema, or both, to give up those precious parts of himself to feed the monster (many children actually think a monster lives in the toilet).

When he is finally able to pass his enlarged, hardened feces, they may tear his tender anal tissues. Physical pain and psychological insults will then forever be unconsciously associated with bowel movements.

The products of his bowel are not viewed by his mother as precious gifts, as they are to him. They are called "dirty," "nasty," and "icky" - waste to be loathed.

As he regards his feces as part of himself, the baby applies those words and attitudes to his essential self, associating anything to do with his bowels as dirty, nasty, sinful, a source of shame and embarrassment. He may try to regain some control over his own body by either withholding (and becoming constipated) or deliberately soiling himself.

Even without the severe treatment, humiliation, and punishment, many children suffer from impatient, angry, anal-retentive, and ignorant parents, who may even batter their children in an effort to bend them to their will in the bathroom.

Some children have even been killed for innocently soiling their pants and inconveniencing or embarrassing their parents.

We must ask: are we more interested in blind obedience than responsibly growing beautiful and unique human beings?

A whole slew of emotional neuroses may be blamed on early incorrect "toilet training." No wonder we have today's social problems!

Controversial Issue

This has implications for colon hydrotherapists. Mentioning a internal cleansing session provokes some people to instant, heated defensiveness. They react as if you had contemptuously suggested they were full of horse manure, unworthy, and there was something fundamentally wrong with them. At the slightest hint, their private and shameful functions will be exposed, and they rush headlong for the exit, never to be seen again!

Very few people are neutral on the issue of their bowels.

Testimonial

I was born with an imperferit anus. In other words there was no anal opening. The lower large intestine was not complete. The doctor performed surgery to create an anal opening. My parents were instructed to hold their fingers in that area so it wouldn't close. My navel protruded and my intestines were pushing against my urinary tract.

I suffered the first years of my life with much pain. I received enemas every day of my life for the first fifteen years. I still became impacted and I had to wear special pants to conceal this problem. I also had no control over my urination.

Finally, when I was fifteen, the doctor wanted to do a colostomy (a bag where fecal matter accumulates instead of a colon).

My parents gave me that choice. I said I've had enough; go through with the surgery. At that time, there was a family friend who was a medical doctor, and he suggested colon hydrotherapy as a last resort before performing the colostomy surgery.

The colon hydrotherapist I went to said "stay on my program for a year and you will be normal." He did not believe my colon was paralyzed as the medical doctors thought.

I began with 3 sessions a week, then two a week, then one a week, then one a month over a period of one year. I didn't have to wear special pants any longer, had no more pain, and the urinary tract went back to normal.

My bowel movements became normal without enemas.

I became a normal, functioning human being, thanks to colon hydrotherapy.

Today I am forty years old, and my bowel movements are still normal.

Steve

Not Out of Gas

An old school chum of mine told me of an incident where she had a "hot" date when she was in her twenties. She was very anxious, as the plan was to go out to dinner to a very elegant restaurant overlooking the ocean.

She dressed up, looking very glamorous. Her date came to the door in his suit, knocked, and then walked her to the car. He opened the door for her, then proceeded to go around to enter the driver's side. As he climbed into the car, he passed gas quite loudly, which destroyed the whole mood of the evening. He said, "Excuse me," but it upset her so much she could not even eat the steak and lobster she ordered at the restaurant. He tried to get a goodnight kiss at the end of the evening, but she could not kiss him. She kept thinking of his gas which completely repulsed her.

Teenagers usually are embarrassed by internal cleansing, while prepubescent children seem to be good patients. At sixteen I was on a date with my first love. We drove by a fertilized lettuce field near Monterey and the smell was putrid. I was terribly embarrassed and neither one of us said a word.

I felt ashamed. How sad.

In today's society, each of us controls our bowels and gas. There is no greater humiliation than publicly having flatulence or soiling oneself. Yet children trained to restrain colon-related opinions can blurt out embarrassing statements.

A client shared she had her date over for a visit. Her niece's five-year-old sat between them, chatting away.

Suddenly, the little girl stopped talking, looked at the man, and in a demanding voice asked, "Did you fart?"

My client was very embarrassed and said, "You should not say that to people!" She then casually commented his breath smelled like flatulence. He had very bad breath.

In everything else, we teach young children to channel their desires to gain social acceptance. But not in this. A basic struggle for control ensues

73

between anal-retentive parents and their beleaguered children, whose bodies rightly belong to themselves and should be self-controlled.

While children must learn when and where it is appropriate to relieve themselves, to force them beyond their capacity, so that they soil themselves, and then punish them is cruel.

In the process of growth and maturation, a child is taught to suppress natural urges. The motivation for success should most often be the reward of wearing underwear or panties like big people.

The negatively "toilet-trained" child grows up to be obsessively private about bowel movements, and will not usually seek out internal cleansing nor accept it if offered.

If absolutely necessary, such a person may privately self-administer an enema. Because of the negative subconscious programming of this person's early "toilet-training" experiences, this psychological barrier is probably the hardest to overcome.

This psychological state cuts across all segments of our society, and includes powerful and successful professionals: doctors, attorneys, politicians, etc..

No one is immune.

I have been on TV talk-shows on numerous occasions discussing internal cleansing and detoxification. Every time, phones ring continuously with people inquiring about internal cleansing. Articles are usually printed in local newspapers: one two-page article was written about me and colon cleansing. After that article appeared, the newspaper received an average of fifty calls a day.

Contrasting society's negative body view is the positively toilet-trained child. This child's parents are aware of their baby's physical, neural, and mental limitations, and do not unduly pressure their child to use the potty.

By about age two, the child usually becomes interested in using the potty like mommy and daddy or older sister or brother. At first the potty is pretty much a toy, but gradually becomes more appropriate for depositing feces. The child is allowed to observe and admire its produce, maybe even carrying it in to show someone important.

The child is praised for producing, never reprimanded, and the parents do not show disgust.

In time, children learn the toilet cannot swallow them, and they lose their fear. They may even help flush their feces away. When big enough, they willingly use the grownup toilet, sometimes with mom or dad steadying them. Mom provides a non-constipating diet.

Children should not associate defecating with shame. Privacy, going behind closed doors, eventually becomes modesty and consideration of others, rather than embarrassment and self-loathing, the need to hide from others the nasty thing being done.

Using appropriate facilities like adults, children learn to relieve themselves as needed. They discover that relieving themselves feels good, and they have the right to feel good about it.

Such children have had a positive toilet-learning experience; they learn bowel movements are not only necessary but also good.

A child positively toilet taught interacts well with others and soon learns the inappropriateness of talking with some people about going "poopie." But if the subject arises with no negative feedback, such a person can quickly achieve a two-year-old level again.

This happens often in internal cleansing. I find positively toilet-taught people confide easily and reach a rapid level of trust with their colon hydrotherapist. Psychologists would do well as colon hydrotherapists; they are often clients.

In any case, positive toilet training is more natural. Bowel movements do give relief. They are, after all, waste products and toxic to us.

Bowel movements do not have to be offensive. Remember, if we eat healthy foods such as vegetables, fruits, grains, legumes, raw nuts and seeds, very little fish, chicken, and turkey, and clean out toxins and old matter, our bowel movements will not smell. Nor, if we have the right balance of lactobacilli and coliform bacilli, will the gas we pass be as offensive.

This is great news! We can defecate in any toilet and not be embarrassed.

Sometimes a negatively toilet-trained person can conquer at least some of early conditioning's trauma. Working through past shame, a person can change; personality blocks are overcome. At last, this poor soul will know the benefits of a clean, healthy body. Internal cleanliness is recognized to have tremendous health benefits.

The spread of bubonic plague, and many other diseases, in the Middle Ages was largely due to the personal filthiness of the day. Clean water was eventually discovered to prevent diseases - typhoid fever, cholera, and diarrhea, among others.

Today, the cleaning of skin, teeth, and hair is a basic prerequisite to participating in society.

Not surprisingly, an act of the body so subject to psychological forces holds important implications for health.

One critical balance in the body is between assimilation of nutrients and elimination of the resulting waste products. It seems, however, our homeostatic systems are usually not quite up to peak efficiency. Like all systems, our elimination process is less than one hundred percent efficient.

Therefore, extra dietary bulk and roughage are vital to health. In addition, as washing the skin seems to have a profound, positive effect on health, so too, and even more so, does the washing of the colon.

It seems other cultures and older ways are wiser than we and could teach us much. It is not so bad to be internally pure.

Colon cancer is the second leading cause of cancer deaths in the United States, annually killing fifty to sixty thousand people!

If we as a society adopted internal cleansing as a second-line (the first being proper diet), disease prevention strategy, many such deaths could be avoided.

We might even look back on today as the Dark Ages of the Industrial-Technological Age!
Yes!

Reluctant M.D.'s

For the present, people just do not want to discuss the colon. Even a number of medical doctors do not really want to talk about it nor listen to patients' complaints about it.

People may find they complain to their M.D.'s of constipation. Their doctors will immediately write a prescription for a laxative, and that would be the last of that subject.

M.D.'s seldom involve themselves with what they feel is an offensive part of the body. Too few seem to recognize the importance of a clean colon. Many find the topic just as offensive as their patients do, having in common conditioning by society. But with enough people learning of and experiencing the extraordinary health benefits of this important therapy, this can change. Become one of these people!

Take Stock of Attitudes

Take stock of your life: are ingrained attitudes keeping you from living the healthy, vital life you were born to live?

I tell those who want good health to seek out a good, certified colon hydrotherapist and get their whole body cleansed and revitalized! Reward one's struggling body for all its efforts to keep going (despite malnourishing it) by giving it the healthy diet it needs and deserves!

Then, like so many folks who have experienced a detoxification and internal cleansing program, one may boldly, daringly share this experience with someone else. You now know the truth and the truth has set you free. You are free to share with someone whom you know also desperately needs internal cleansing.

CHAPTER FOUR

CONTROVERSY OF INTERNAL CLEANSING

Internal cleansing is controversial because it deals with the colon, which, as we saw in the previous chapter, is a taboo subject in our society. It is also controversial because it is not supported and is basically ignored by the medical establishment.

Consequently, internal cleansing is regarded as little more than shamanism or blood-letting by leeches.

Did you know that the word "leech" is the old Middle English/Anglo-Saxon origin of our word "doctor?" "Leechcraft" is the practice of medicine; "lecch" is "doctor!"

The majority of our society is not aware of internal cleansing's existence. The problem is that though no officially recognized research supports this type of therapy, no research questions or condemns it either. It languishes in health-care limbo.

Popular thinking goes, "If a medical treatment is not acclaimed in a prestigious medical or research journal, it cannot be good."

Until recently, controversy has muzzled official bans of the procedure. But no one, it seems, can negate colon hydrotherapy's position.

Exceptional Cases

A report from the Center for Disease Control that was first published on March 31, 1981, in which patients supposedly died from colon hydrotherapy, failed to acknowledge that patient deaths were due to surgical complications. When their doctors cut them open to treat the affected sites, they inadvertently perforated the colons and caused the development of peritonitis.

One problem was corrected, but another was created.

The two people who did not undergo surgery did not die.

To bolster their argument against colon hydrotherapy, misguided detractors cite other reports involving rare cases of bowel perforations resulting from incorrectly given enemas. As stated before, these cases were with infants and mental patients in hospitals.

On a few occasions, home enemas, made from fatally toxic mixtures of household cleaners, have been administered by overzealous parents to their constipated or ill children. Of these cases, some resulted in water-intoxication and death.

This sad reliance on exceptional and irrelevant examples demonstrates the depth of the medical establishment's ignorance, even among specialists in the fields of gastroenterology and oncology.

For the establishment, internal cleansing remains misunderstood. In the first place, distinctions between colon hydrotherapy and enema usage are fuzzy. In the second place, internal cleansing's practical therapeutic applications go unrecognized, and state-of-the-art procedures and equipment go under-utilized.

How Many Sessions?

In interviews with doctors and health practitioners regarding internal cleansing, I was surprised to hear many say that people need only three sessions of colon hydrotherapy.

The reasons given were:

1.) "Too much colon-cleansing can be habit-forming."

2.) "People become dependent upon colon-cleansings like they do laxatives."

3.) "You will detox and cleanse the colon completely with three treatments."

Nothing can be further from the truth. On the contrary, the reverse happens.

I stated earlier that the colon is a muscular organ often impacted with stool. When the colon is unburdened and exercised, it works more efficiently. I have seen this happen time and again.

My question to one doctor was, "Have you ever seen any instances of colon hydrotherapy becoming habit-forming and the bowel not being able to evacuate as a result?"

His answer was, "No."

He had only given his opinion without providing any facts. Another health practitioner stated that a person only needed three colon cleansing sessions.

"Why?" I asked.

He stated that three sessions were sufficient to clean out the colon.

This again is simply not true.

My thirteen years of practicing internal cleansing have shown that to thoroughly detoxify and clean the colon, a minimum of ten treatments is necessary. To assert that shorter treatment suffices is similar in concept to the assertion that a seven-day fast completely cleans the body. Yet, Paul Bragg, author of *Miracle of Fasting*, observed a twenty-one-day fast, and it was not until the eighteenth day that he passed DDT and other poisons from urination.

A Doctor's Orders

Once, a medical doctor referred a cancer patient to me. The man was suffering from constipation, which was caused by medications he was taking to combat his disease. He was, unfortunately, in the last stages of this illness.

Gently, I gave him colon hydrotherapy which washed out some of the impacted matter from his lower colon. He felt slight relief, and, as he was to return home back east the next day, I bade him good-bye, thinking I would probably never hear from him again.

His colon's arrested peristalsis had been stimulated by the cleansing and was trying, naturally, to move out even more of the stool left in the rest of his bowel.

He began suffering abdominal cramps.

By the time his plane landed, the cramping was painful enough for his wife to take him to the hospital. The doctors took a report from him, asking what had happened to him in the last twenty-four hours. He told them he had received colon hydrotherapy.

They diagnosed his problem as a perforated bowel, resulting from the colon cleansing.

In a panic, the cancer-sufferer's wife called the doctor in San Diego who had referred the patient to me. She hysterically explained what had transpired. Coincidentally, I was working in the referring doctor's office, so I answered the phone and caught the brunt of the poor woman's frustration, fear, and anger.

Even as I sympathized, all I could imagine was a huge lawsuit. I knew I had done nothing harmful, but with the medical prejudices against internal cleansing, I did not believe I would have a chance.

I could not understand it; when he left my office, this sick man had been feeling so much better!

The M.D. who had referred the patient to me called the hospital, identified himself with his medical credentials, and asked to speak to the diagnosing doctors.

He explained that he had prescribed the colon hydrotherapy. After talking with this M.D., the hospital's doctors CHANGED THEIR DIAGNOSIS. The man was given treatment for his exaggerated symptoms, and all turned out well.

This incident was not caused by the hospital doctors' ignorance. They knew the cancer victim did not have a perforated colon.

But because of prejudice, they decided to blame colon hydrotherapy.

The diagnosis was retracted only when it was found out a fellow M.D. had prescribed treatment. Otherwise, the previous diagnosis would have stuck. No one would have known any different. The establishment could have said anything it wanted, and no one could have questioned it.

The reader should note that after administering approximately 17,000 treatments of internal cleansing, not ONE of my clients has ever experienced a perforated colon or any other problem resulting from internal cleansing!

Unnatural Treatment?

Another objection from the establishment to internal cleansing is that the procedure is "unnatural." Yet, even in our natural state, we, as human beings, are, of all Nature's creatures, wholly unnatural.

Homes, apartments, cottages, and cardboard shacks are not natural.

Cooking food - whether over a fire, in an oven, a microwave, on a stove-top, or having it served to you in a restaurant is not natural.

Using telephones, computers, typewriters, and adding machines is not natural.

If you use rest rooms and their facilities - toilets and urinals - you are being unnatural,

If you take prescription chemical drugs for diagnosed symptoms, you are unnatural.

If you are in an accident and get medicine, care, stitches, broken bones set, or surgery, you are absolutely unnatural.

The most unnatural thing that people do these days is eat unnatural foods: foods that have all the good fiber processed out; foods in which enzymes necessary for vitamin and mineral assimilation are destroyed through cooking; flesh foods; pasteurized and homogenized dairy products; foods that have harmful hormones, chemicals, dyes, additives, preservatives, pesticides, and chemical fertilizers.

Supposedly, the medical community considers our diet to be wholly and completely natural for human beings.

Get the picture?

That medical doctors can even protest unorthodox therapeutic practices such as colon hydrotherapy is unnatural.

When something goes wrong among our physiological systems, we have the capability to fix it internally or get outside help. This is why we have remedies, therapies, and doctors.

Thus the pseudo-argument against the "unnaturalness" of internal cleansing falls apart. The people performing the most unnatural of procedures - pouring and popping unnatural chemicals, in the form of syrups and pills, down the throats of unwell patients; cutting people open and rearranging or removing internal body parts; making surgical patients sleep an unnatural sleep under unnatural and dangerous chemical anesthesia - are those protesting that internal cleansing is "unnatural."

All this because internal cleansing simply and gently puts warm sterilized water into and out of human colons.

Does that make sense?

There is something very wrong here.

Television Broadcast

The following statements were made on a televised report on health, with news anchor Jim Wilkerson reporting. Various medical experts gave their opinions as to current health information.

Earl Mendell, vitamin author, states:

Doctors state that we need milk for strong bones. Really?

Five studies show that the five leading nations consuming the most milk daily have the highest incidence of osteoporosis, while nations consuming no dairy products have no osteoporosis.

In recent years, the agriculture department has announced a new shape for the ideal diet. Instead of the familiar pie chart of the so-called basic food groups, the new shape is a pyramid emphasizing grains and not much fat.

It is no wonder there is so much confusion. It is said that only a third of the medical schools require students to study nutrition. Courses in preventive medicine, nutrition and exercise are seldom taught in our nation's medical schools. Instead, medical students are subjected to course after course on pharmacology. They are taught that drugs are some of the more useful tools for treating disease.

No one wants to tell Americans they are lazy and set in their ways, or that they cry too easily to doctors when they get sick, leaving an unpayable $800 billion medical bill. On the one hand, people cry because no one takes care of them, and, on the other hand, they are not willing themselves to prevent disease.

People must take charge of their own health.

Mendell also states, *"We spend 97% of our health care dollars on sickness and only 3% on prevention."*

On the same broadcast, Dr. Gary Knoll, author and medical reporter, states, *"We are the sickest nation in the world. We have the highest medical bill in the world. We eat the worst food in the world and yet we have the best food in the world, we're just not eating it."*

News anchor Jim Wilkerson reported:

"The purest foods are available in the health food stores, and the government strangles them by considering legislation that would make vitamins and herbs prescription only. So, we're looking at the safest industry in the free world, the industry of nutritional supplements, yet the FDA wants to regulate that industry out of existence. It is the safest industry we have. It is totally insane.

It is time we take control of our own bodies!

A recent cover story of Time magazine told how new research has shown that vitamins may help fight cancer, heart disease, and aging. The article claimed that "only 9 percent of the American people eat well enough to get all their nutrients from foods." I called the FDA in Washington and got phonebounced four times until, finally, I got to a guy who would take my questions about chelation, tryptophane, and about the health food industry, and he said he would mail me a position paper that very day.

And that was more than two weeks ago. I haven't received a thing.

Prevention is of primary importance.

In a news story regarding health, Dr. Gary Noll states:

> *The basic four food groups concept is a fraud, an absolute fraud. It is voodoo science, it is witchcraft, it is the worst abomination. It's what's killing us. We have the most tyrannical bureaucracy in the world in the form of the FDA. There is no limit on alcohol or tobacco we can put into our body, but they want to cut back on the amount of nutrients we can have that can be prevention.*

Julian Wittacher, M.D., states, *"Bypass surgery, for instance, has failed miserably."* He cites two government-funded, controlled studies to establish long term benefits of prevention, and he showed supported studies from the AMA.

> *"In the list of facts doctors cannot tell their patients, but want them to know, doctors are terrified of two things: "malpractice suits and being labeled non-conformist."*

> *The doctors' job is not to keep them well, but to help them after they get sick. The more costly the procedure, tests and drugs, the more the system makes. The crisis intervention of medicine and the use of aggressive therapies in many cases when they are not warranted is bankrupting the country."*

Dr. Wittacher has investigated the medical profession for twenty years and has written dozens of books. He writes:

> *I worked with Dr. Pritigen back in 1976, and I saw large numbers of people get well. Yet, when I was in medical school and medical training, I never saw anybody get well. I saw people get better. I saw people get out of the hospital with their prescription, and many came back, and we never really learn how to make people well. I think that it is time that the American public realize the FDA is not necessarily looking out for your best interest.*

They're on their own, because no one in the American system has the guts to say to the American people 'Change or die.'

Earl Mendell, on Channel 10 News, states:

The government has already killed tryptophane. You do not see it here. Four years ago some people died after taking the popular natural sleep inducing amino acid. But investigation proved it was a tainted batch from Japan, but tryptophane is still banned.

I think it was working too well, and I think it was starting to hurt the sale of other drugs. It's interesting that they had a tainted Tylenol. In two days, it is back on the market.

Pill Therapy vs. Internal cleansing

Some fear unknown side effects from internal cleansing. To many, as we saw in Chapter Three, discussions of body elimination can be repulsive. This may be one reason why pill therapy this century has been so embraced by doctors and their patients alike.

The solution pills offer seems simple, neat, and fast acting. However, pill therapy falls short of the mark. While in many cases the main effect of medication seems nothing short of miraculous, many drugs carry side effects that may turn out to be more devastating than the symptoms they were intended to treat. In addition, pill therapy leaves the body in a toxic state. Remember, pills treat the symptoms, not the cause.

Despite this knowledge, doctors continue to prescribe medications. They may or may not briefly discuss possible side effects with the patient, but gloss over negative possibilities to alleviate patient anxiety. For, in terms of time and effort, it inconveniences a doctor when a patient balks at taking medication and takes the doctor's valuable time to inquire about all the information regarding the prescription.

Beware of Drugs' Side Effects

Side effects should not be overlooked.

Indeed, when you get a prescription, usually enclosed is a tightly folded page listing the drug's "contraindications." The text is in such tiny print you may legitimately wonder if you were intended to read it. These "contraindications" are known side effects associated with the medication. The literature details their seriousness, the conditions under which they occur, and results of related experiments. The wording is dry and clinical, often unintelligible to the lay reader, so as not to arouse alarm.

Doctors may expect patients to take medication on an ongoing basis, not knowing if patients will show recognized symptoms of side effects or how particular bodies will react to certain drugs.

In the event a patient reacts negatively, the doctor will make one of two choices: to adjust the dosage and see what happens, or discontinue that medication and try another one. Even after all the clinical testing of a medication, the patient is still a guinea pig, because everyone's body differs in its chemical interactions.

Ironically, the same doctors who knowingly prescribe medications with possibly known deleterious side effects caution against internal cleansing because of its possible "unknown" side effects!

This, despite there being absolutely NONE on record anywhere. Again, these doctors try to hide behind an old smokescreen. They maintain there are no "scientific, peer-reviewed" studies to document the safety of internal cleansing.

Clearly, the medical establishment is not about to begin a study! Who knows what acute or long-term damage is taking place while many are taking prescription drugs? And these medications may lead to complications that have no corrective recourse.

An example of just such a complication is a condition known as "dry mouth," which occurs as a side effect of over four hundred prescription drugs. It is usually discovered by dentists attempting to treat patients complaining of this symptom. Because the salivary glands fail to secrete enough saliva (which contains digestive enzymes that kill many harmful bacteria, thus keeping the enamel-eating bacteria neutralized), patients tend to experience an increase in the number of dental cavities.

Hooked on Colonics?

Another protest from ignorant but vocal medical personnel is that internal cleansing can be "addictive" or habit-forming. There has not been one case I know of where a person cannot have a bowel movement without a colonic.

Just the opposite is true.

Those with severe constipation are inversely helped in overcoming this condition.

The other dependency cited as a possibility is based on a primary misunderstanding of what internal cleansing actually is.

Most opponents fuzzily equate internal cleansing with a laxative.

This assumption is erroneous!

Laxatives use chemicals irritating to the lining of the colon, making it convulse defensively. When laxatives are used too much, the natural peristalsis of the colon, weakened by constipation to begin with, desists entirely, and the body must then wait for the laxative to stimulate contraction of the colon's muscles. In time, increasing amounts of the laxative are required to obtain the desired result. This condition is dangerous for obvious reasons, and is in reality a chemical dependence.

There are about three hundred varieties of laxatives. They are the number two drug sold in the U.S.A.

I would say this country has an uptight anus!

Ultimate Goal of Internal Cleansing

Basically, the colon is like an old water pipe. It keeps getting more sluggish and flaccid from daily ingestion of the wrong foods.

I believe we take better care of our cars than we do our bodies.

We change the oil and lubricate our autos at the recommended times because we want our cars to last longer, without expense later.

However, how often do we clean out the digestive system where sewage lies stagnating?

How can we expect to live long, healthy, and energetic lives if we do not clean out the build-up put in by destructive living habits?

In contrast to laxatives, colon hydrotherapy "jump-starts" a sluggish colon into renewed peristaltic vigor!

Over time, an unresponsive colon is stimulated into natural peristaltic action by the gentle introduction and evacuation of water, cleansing of its clogged passageway. Normal peristaltic action to eliminate a normal waste load can be reestablished. Since colon hydrotherapy uses only water - no drugs - no type of chemical dependency can develop. Period.

After cleaning out the overburdened, constipated, or non-functioning colon, the natural peristalsis is restored; so the colon can resume normal operation on its own, unassisted.

This, in fact, is the ultimate goal of internal cleansing!

Therapy Could Have Saved Elvis

When Elvis Presley died, the world was shocked. The idol of millions was an unnaturally bloated, unhealthy, and unhappy man. Rumor has it that his autopsy supposedly revealed thirty-two pounds of impacted fecal matter in his colon. Regularly taking many prescription drugs, some incompatible, and suffering evident chronic constipation - caused in part by the medications - caused his untimely and needless death. He died in the bathroom.

I believe, based on countless similar cases, that if Elvis had cleansed his bowels with colon hydrotherapy, gone on a program of a juice fast and cleansing herbs, and then changed his diet, he would be a vigorously alive man today. I also believe his deepening depression was caused partly by bad diet and a malfunctioning colon. The prescription drugs were intended to help, but only exacerbated his condition. His doctors tried everything they knew, but Elvis died anyway - of ignorance.

Electrolyte Depletion?

It is argued that colon hydrotherapy sessions can deplete a patient's electrolytes. This, however, was disproved by a study at the National Homeopathic College.

Electrolytes are vital to health and life, and are instantly replaced by eating. A good suggestion would be to drink a glass of whole, natural fruit juice.

Fear of electrolyte depletion is inapplicable in arguments against colon hydrotherapy. This objection can only be used by one ignorant in the realities of the therapy.

Doctors have objected to internal cleansing as an invasive procedure; however, is not brushing our teeth an invasive procedure, or getting a tattoo, or douching, or putting a Q-tip in your ears, or inserting a suppository?

Medical doctors oftentimes cannot guarantee positive results from their invasive procedures. On the other hand, qualified colon hydrotherapists can be sure their clients receive gentle treatment and will only gain overall health benefits. People who come to colon hydrotherapists never need fear the risks associated with most orthodox medical practices.

AB 856 Controversy

Regardless of the benefits clients experience, internal cleansing still faces discrimination from the medical community. Particularly troublesome and puzzling was one reaction from a small group of M.D.'s. The only explanation was, perhaps, egoism and greed.

The following is an example of misinformation.

In December of 1991, Mr. Ken Douglas of the Medical Board of California received this letter from a former president of the California Medical

Association, Laurens P. White, M.D., Internal Medicine and Oncology, of San Francisco:

Dear Mr. Douglas:

I am writing you to put on paper my statement to you that the performance of colonic irrigation, a practice clearly condemned by the medical and by the chiropractic professions, is very much an element of the practice of medicine which has been outlawed. I know of no reputable physicians or chiropractors who perform this procedure any longer.

Colonic irrigation (or flushing) has been outlawed for several good reasons. These are:

1) It has no useful therapeutic functions.

2) Whether done with water, coffee or liquids, it is without benefit.

3) It is dangerous, and may result in rupture of the bowel, peritonitis or unusual fluid absorption.

For these reasons no one should perform this disreputable pseudo-therapy, and anyone performing it should be considered guilty of unprofessional conduct.

Yours truly, Laurens P. White, M.D.

As you can probably see right off, non sequiturs and false statements fill this letter. It would seem the good doctor did not read well whatever sources he consulted, and evidently was not aware of the differences between enemas and colon hydrotherapy. In fact, he probably had never known any recipient of colon hydrotherapy or known a colon hydrotherapist.

The White letter was snatched up by Assemblywoman Tricia Hunter, who had once been a nurse. She apparently saw this letter as an opportunity to produce legislation in the California State Assembly, and introduced Assembly Bill 856. As if by way of endorsement of her actions, the California Medical Association was the largest contributor to Hunter's re-election campaign, chipping in with a whopping $12,500.

Leslie Williams noted the following in a response to Hunter's AB 856:

The California Secretary of State, March Fong Eu's files... [revealed that] Tricia Hunter received a check for $5,000 from the CMA on April 8, 1992, the day before the bill was introduced and a second check for $7,500... a month later, on May 9, 1992.

First, except for chiropractors, there is, in fact, no California law against obtaining or administering colon hydrotherapy. The therapy is not "an element of the practice of medicine which has been outlawed."

Second, if "no reputable physicians or chiropractors... perform this procedure any longer," why the necessity for a law?

Third, if it has "no useful therapeutic function" and "is without benefit," why worry about it? Drinking fourteen glasses of water instead of the recommend eight has no useful therapeutic function and probably no greater benefit than the recommended dose, yet it will not hurt, either. Should we outlaw drinking more water than the recommended eight glasses per day?

Fourth, there are NO reported cases of ruptured bowels, peritonitis, or unusual fluid absorption due to colon hydrotherapy in over 150 years anywhere in the United States of America! There are, however, such cases due to improperly administered enemas.

Fact: Since internal cleansing became a "profession" in the middle of the last century (1800s) in North America, there have been no reports of injuries. The one case cited by **AB 856** in Colorado was amoeba contamination.

Colon hydrotherapy is normally such a benign procedure that it seems even when sterilization, procedural techniques, and equipment were not so advanced, it still was not a threat to anyone's health.

Out of millions of internal cleansing sessions performed, only those in Colorado in 1981 - under the surgeon's knife - died. Such a casualty rate over the last century is an enviable record for any area of professional medicine.

The one incident that has been cited as a reason to outlaw colon hydrotherapy occurred over 25 years ago. It had nothing to do with the therapy or the technique of administration. But it involved a tank and reusable hose that was joined together away from the body. Unfortunately, the person using the equipment did not bother to change the hoses between sessions, allowing the following client to be infected with the previous client's contaminants. When a client who suffered from amoebic dysentery came in for several sessions, 33 people were infected through the unsanitary hoses.

Leslie Williams, then President of the International Association for Colon Hydrotherapists states the following:

No one died after getting colon hydrotherapy. Those that died did so after bowel surgery performed by the medical doctors. The session itself did not cause any illness. It was the unsanitary conditions where the patients contracted amoebas.

Gregory Istre, MD, wrote an article in the *New England Journal of Medicine* on the spread of amoebiasis via colon hydrotherapy. He was interviewed by Leslie Williams. He told her he was "surprised that [the] California Medical Association used this article to try to outlaw a whole profession."

This legislation was carried by then Assembly woman Tricia Hunter from the Palm Springs area. It was introduced April 9, 1992 in the middle of the second half of the legislative two-year term. Within a week of the bill, being discovered, the legislator's offices in the Capital in Sacramento, California resounded with phone calls, letters, and personal visits. The unfortunate assemblyman who had co-authored the bill before it was gutted and replaced with the new legislation hurriedly removed his name from the bill. He had no knowledge of the change and his clerical staff was overwhelmed by the number of indignant callers demanding that the piece be dropped. The staff felt they should be answering the phone "hydrotherapy central!" One of the staff members of a Senator on the health

94

committee marveled that of the thousands of bills introduced each legislative session, none had created the furor that this one had, other than one concerning water rights due to the drought.

The bill had one hearing, then was tabled, due to lack of documented proof of causing harm.

In 1984, a chiropractor in San Diego, John Luly, advertised internal cleansing as a cure for various ailments. The California Medical Board sued him, and after years in court, the judge ruled that although internal cleansing had been a part of the chiropractor's scope of practice in California, he ruled against the chiropractor, and in the future, chiropractors could no longer administer colon hydrotherapy.

At that, the Chiropractic Examining Board sued the California Medical Association to establish that chiropractors could indeed perform internal cleansing. This was paid for out of public funds allocated by the Attorney General. This suit lasted seven years and cost two million dollars of taxpayer money. Cause and effect of internal cleansing was not attempted to be determined. It was simply a turf war. The end result appeared that the chiropractors were going to lose, so they dropped the suit and agreed to back legislation outlawing the procedure as a concession to pressure from the California Medical Association.

The C.M.A. wrote the proposed assembly bill, thinking, no doubt, it had a no-contest case, and that the bill would pass without anyone's awareness, since the general populace is fairly unaware of the existence and benefits of internal cleansing (as are most member doctors in the C.M.A.).

AB 856 Controversy Continues

For a field so obscure as internal cleansing, the outcry was loud. Only two interests supported **AB 856**: the C.M.A. and (California) Board of Chiropractic Examiners. This second group had lost its battle to practice internal cleansing to the C.M.A. after a heroic seven-year battle in the 1980's. On the other side of the battle line were nine groups and countless individuals, 265 of whom went on record with letters of protest to the California State Senate Health and Human Services Committee.

The groups opposed to AB 856 were:
American Colon Therapist Association
California Colon Therapy Society
Specialty Health Products
Laguna Medical Center, Inc.
Wellness Associates
Dotolo Research Corporation
Church of the Golden Light
California Nurses Association
California Chiropractic Association

MD's Speak Out For Internal Cleansing

Medical Doctors were among those individuals who cared enough and took the time to write to their state representatives.

Ron Kennedy, an M.D. from Rohnert Park, California, wrote Senate Health and Human Services Committee Chairperson Diane Watson a one-and-a-half page letter explaining that he had studied internal cleansing for two years and had "come to the conclusion that it is a valuable procedure which, in trained hands, is as safe as any procedure performed on the human body can be."

He stated that he also thought it "extremely useful as a method of preventing serious colon disease." He recommended that if any regulatory action be taken that it be along the lines of Florida policy, which licenses internal cleansing as an adjunct to massage therapy.

Dr. Kennedy pointed out that medical schools provide no training in internal cleansing, and that medical physicians are "trained to handle the body after disease is present and perhaps even life threatening." He went on to make a remarkable statement, considering he himself is a medical doctor, "[Physicians] have little interest, as a group, in prevention of illness."

In another paper, Kennedy writes:
In my view it would be unconstitutional to outlaw the practice of colonics by colon

96

therapists and leave it to medical doctors who know next to nothing about the prevention of colon disease.

Most colon therapists are convinced, as I certainly am, that the great increase in colon cancer over the past few generations is also due to autointoxication in the colon. High fiber foods change the bacterial flora of your colon to non-carcinogenic organisms and drastically reduce the possibility of colon cancer.

Medical doctors are simply not trained to deal with the colon until it becomes severely diseased. I tell my clients the prevention of disease begins with an internal cleansing program. This is invaluable.

A client told me she went to the doctor and asked about some mucus she saw in her bowel movement. She wondered why he replied that the discharge came not from her bowel but from her vagina. I, too, wondered why the doctor did not seem to know mucus is found numerous times in pieces of stool.

In his work, Dr. Kennedy concludes that putrefying waste material causes autointoxication and leads to dangerous pre-cancerous conditions in the colon. In addition, various other gastrointestinal complaints and diseases are associated with a poisoned bowel.

Kennedy connects the effects of toxicity to other ailments seemingly unrelated to the bowel. In his view, these are problems which, because of ignorance of a sick bowel as the root cause, medical doctors of all specialties find difficult to treat successfully.

This will be discussed in more detail in Chapter Six. Another opponent of **AB 856**, John W. Travis, M.D., M.P.H., of Sebastopol, CA, wrote the following to Chairperson Watson:

I'm shocked at the apparent attempt to outlaw colon hydrotherapy via AB 856. While I do not practice it myself, I believe it is one of many important forms of treatment that we were not taught in medical school... I hope you and your committee will provide the much needed leadership to prevent such regressive legislation from occurring.

In agreement, Bessie Jo Tillman, M.D., of Redding, also wrote to the committee:

I frequently refer [constipated] patients for colon [hydro]therapy... I have never had problems with serious injuries and illnesses, such as infection, bowel perforation, bowel necrosis (death of the bowel tissues caused by use of caustic soaps or other irritants that attack the delicate lining of the colon) and death with the sophisticated and refined temperatures and pressure gauges, disposable tubing and speculum and trained certified therapists... I have only obtained positive results. I have never had complaints.

Elson M. Haas, M.D., director of a clinic in San Rafael, states that in over fifteen years of referring patients to colon hydrotherapists for treatment, he has "never seen any medical complications... in over hundreds of patients."

He goes on to explain the safety and efficacy of modern internal cleansing practices, and ultimately maintains, "there is essentially no risk of medical problems. The statements in the current Assembly Bill 856 about the hazards of colon [hydrotherapy] are simply erroneous."

And again, "[This] simple procedure cannot cause bowel necrosis and death, and in well-trained hands with proper techniques there is no risk of infection and bowel perforation."

Paul Lynn, M.D., of San Francisco, had this to say to the Senate Health and Human Services Committee:

I feel that this form of natural health care is falsely represented and that the information in the upcoming Assembly Bill 856 regarding these procedures is totally inaccurate by claiming them harmful and dangerous.

I have frequently referred patients to get [internal cleansing] from a qualified therapist [who] uses proven sophisticated equipment including a refined pressure gauge along with disposable tubing. I have received only positive reports from these sessions and if it were not safe and sanitary, I would not recommend them. I urge you to reconsider this unconstitutional bill from being passed into law.

This sampling shows the outcry from an informed segment of the medical community.

A number of celebrities were unafraid to make a public stand for the practice of internal cleansing. In fact, many movie stars who regularly receive internal cleansing submitted letters to Senators and Assemblymen protesting the passage of **AB 856**.

A Biased Doctor Responds

At the other end of the spectrum, the C.M.A.'s Frederick H. Noteware, Assistant Director of Government Relations, wrote in support of AB 856 to the C.M.A.'s "expert" witness, President Richard F. Corlin, M.D.:

I am taking this opportunity to pass along to you those comments I have received from those who advocate the administration of colonic irrigations:

1. From Nancy McBride, chiropractor: "If a person needs an enema, they certainly need a colonic irrigation."

"Why?"

"Because the body gets toxic."

"What does that mean?"

"There's feedback into the liver."

2. There are people who consider themselves to be "colon therapists" after having received training and certification at some as yet unnamed institution. I'm beginning to hear what they may suggest as a compromise... amend AB 856 (Hunter) to create a new category of licensure for colon therapists. I have explained this would be absolutely unacceptable for a variety of reasons, not the least of which is the fact the administration of a colonic irrigation is an invasive procedure, and under the law (with few exceptions), only physicians and surgeons may perform invasive procedures. My view is if the "colon therapists" offer licensure as a compromise, it supports our position since they are acknowledging the inherent value in protecting the public health from untrained practitioners.

3. When asked why colonics are necessary, the common response is usually "to remove the toxins."

4. When pressed as to the therapeutic value, the answer is,

"Well, they make you feel better." I always follow that answer with the question, "Can you provide me with any documented, peer-reviewed, scientific literature to suggest any medical reason to drain the colon?" The answer is always no.

5. Other comments: a. "Physicians do not receive any nutritional training so they wouldn't know the benefits of colon therapy."

b. "Wheat grass enemas have been especially helpful with cancer patients."

c. "This is a freedom of choice issue with my body."

d. "This bill is self-serving by the C.M.A. and motivated by money interests."

The arrogance and laziness of AB 856's supporters within the C.M.A. become apparent with this cynical letter by Noteware. There is no attempt to dig deeper than the surface.

Noteware might not have written such a frivolous and contemptuous recommendation if he had an open mind, performed an unbiased review of the literature, contacted any internal cleansing association, used up some shoe leather to personally interview and observe both practitioners and their clients, or talked to the doctors who prescribe the procedure.

But the gilded status accorded the mere fact of a medical degree in anything - however strong or weak the actual qualifying marks to receive it - seems to have blinded Mr. Noteware to his own erroneous assumptions!

Dr. Corlin, evidently busy as he was, did not subsequently take the time, either, to find out the facts about internal cleansing before he was scheduled to testify to the HHS Committee. Inexplicably, he neglected to clarify to himself the difference between an enema and colon hydrotherapy.

The transcript of the hearing itself is a testimony to arrogant ignorance. Neither Hunter nor Corlin were able to present a satisfactory case for **AB 856**, and only succeeded in frustrating and wearying the Committee by refusing to differentiate between enemas and colon hydrotherapy.

Members of the committee asked for substantiation that the therapy is dangerous, ineffective, or useless.

Interestingly, Corlin could not provide it.

Members of the Committee made reference to the mail they had received on this issue, and even admitted to some personal knowledge of the procedure and its beneficial outcome. One Committee member, Senator Mello, used the example of tonsillectomy to illustrate he was not convinced the medical establishment automatically and infallibly knows everything at any time about any aspect of health.

Corlin was not pleased by these disclosures. They left with their tail between their legs.

The Death of AB 856

The upshot of the hearing was defeat for Hunter's bill. As Chairperson Senator Watson stated, **AB 856** was full of "loopholes big enough to drive a Mack Truck through." She advised Assemblywoman Hunter to take the bill back to the drawing board, and, if it merited it, present it again another time.

AB 856 was not passed that July, 1992.

Since that time, CMA has not been in communication with the I.A.C.T., nor has it pursued any efforts to outlaw colon hydrotherapy.

A.M.A. Forced to Cover Backside

In fact, in recent decades the medical community has provided several such examples of wrong-thinking.

Until the late 1970's, despite studies that clearly showed otherwise, the medical establishment denied any connection between heart disease, diet, and exercise. In the early 1980's, the public demanded an accounting, but instead of acknowledging the error, the A.M.A. simply issued its own authoritative guidelines for heart health.

A.M.A. doctors implied as if they themselves had known and practiced the new approach all along!

A similar tactic was used on the issue of high blood pressure; that battle for patient participation and self-care is still ongoing.

Smoking took a parallel route, except that the tobacco companies overtly and covertly influenced the medical establishment - and still do!

In the sixties, a TV comedy sketch depicted a scene in which a patient (a smoker), hacking and coughing miserably, goes to see his doctor. The doctor has him sit on the examining table, and, with ear to stethoscope, has the patient take a deep breath.

As he does so, the doctor, himself smoking an extra long cigarette, goes into a lengthy spasm of coughing. The patient takes the stethoscope out of the doctor's limp hand and has the doctor sit up on the examining table; whereupon, the patient proceeds to listen to the doctor's chest and recommends that the physician quit smoking!

Until the Surgeon General's announcement that smoking unequivocally causes cancer and emphysema, doctors were actually touting the health benefits of smoking!

To this day, tobacco companies deny that smoking is detrimental to health. They still conduct research at their own labs to try to refute what has been proven fact by many independent studies for over twenty years.

Medical doctors are employed by these tobacco companies to do this research. These are physicians who should know better and are betraying public trust, their training, and all they believe!

Ironically, doctors maintain that they are on the side of freedom of choice. These are the same doctors who would deny colon hydrotherapists the right to perform a procedure with NO deleterious health effects, a method of treatment which is, by all indications, a vital tool in promoting optimal health, as a FREE CHOICE to their patients.

Take Charge of Personal Health

But unless more physicians and their patients are educated about internal cleansing and its real health benefits, it is likely someone in the medical establishment will again try to rob the populace of this legitimate health option.

Knowledge is victory over victimization and illness. Individuals must seek out their own best health! They must take control over their own bodies.

People can begin today to live in optimum health through colon cleansing, cleansing herbs, and proper diet.

This can be done only if one takes the appropriate steps. Hundreds and hundreds of phone calls bombarded the senators and assemblymen. No one had any idea so many people in California receive colon hydrotherapy. In San Diego county alone, a guess is approximately fifteen hundred people a month undergo treatment.

As George Hamilton, the timelessly handsome and health-conscious actor, said in his letter to the Senate Health and Human Services Committee, "I feel that we should all take responsibility for our own health and well-being and that alternative medicine should be available so that we can make that choice."

Two Cases of Successfully Explored Options

These testimonies were written to me as follows:

103

In November, 1988, I was experiencing abdominal pain every day. It was very difficult to work or sleep at night.

After a month of pain, I decided to go to the doctor. He put me on a lactose-free diet. I tried that for a couple of weeks, but that did not help at all.

After running further tests, my doctor still could not find anything wrong with me.

I experienced the pains throughout Christmas. I could not eat because the pain was so bad.

The last day of the year I went to get colon hydrotherapy. I did not notice much difference at first, but one morning soon after, when I woke up, the pains had disappeared and they never returned after that.

Paul

Another testimony is from a lady named Louisa. She wrote to me:

Before internal cleansing, I had trouble sleeping. I could not think clearly or talk to people. I lost my train of thought. I had discomfort and pain in my abdomen. I did a series of treatments along with the cleansing program.

Now I sleep well, think more quickly, and talk with ease. My pain is gone and I can digest foods much better than before.

Taking Control of Our Bodies

It is terribly sad that we are conditioned in this country not to explore alternative health measures. Too often, a grim diagnosis causes us to give up, rather than pursuing the healing available to us from non-conventional sources.

For instance, one out of every four Americans will be diagnosed with cancer. Cancer causes one death in the United States every ninety seconds.

Regarding another disease, the book *2001 Fascinating Facts*, reports:

As of 1977 diabetes was the third leading cause of death by disease in the United States.

It has increased 50 percent since 1965, and today affects at least 10 million Americans. Of the 32 million Americans admitted to hospitals each year, some 1.5 million develop some disease that comes simply from being in the hospital. More than 15,000 people die of such a disease each year. So prevalent is this syndrome that doctors have given it a name - nosocomial disease, from the Greek word nosconium, meaning "hospital."

But there is a wide body of evidence to suggest that these diseases can be combated by internal cleansing and diet!

2001 Fascinating Facts again states:

In ancient China, doctors [were] paid when their patients were kept well, not when they were sick. Believing that it was the doctor's job to prevent disease. Chinese doctors often paid the patient if the patient lost his health. Further, if a patient died, a special lantern was hung outside the doctor's house. At each death another lantern was added. Too many of these lanterns were certain to ensure a slow trade.

This unique custom would certainly give this country a healthy shaking up! Think of the billions of dollars that would be saved, and the pain and suffering that would be eliminated!

My mother and father were both diabetics, as are my sister and my aunts. At this writing, I am fifty-six years old, and I am not a diabetic.

In 1972, I was diagnosed as being border-line diabetic. Today, after many fasts and cleansings, I eat raw honey and barley malt for sweetening. I drink fruit juices and yet do not have any symptoms of diabetes.

Doctors state that if both parents are diabetic, their child will become diabetic.

That is simply not true.

No one has to be anything but a healthy, younger-looking, and vibrant individual. Just because certain tendencies are in the genes does not doom one to destruction.

105

You can be what you want to be!

You can take control of your body and rule it. It does not have to rule you. Believe me, if I can do it, anyone can do it!

Testing the Wrong Option:
A Study of Hyperactive Children

A recent study tested two groups of hyperactive children. One group was fed a concentrated sugar diet. The other group was given food sweetened with cyclamates and saccharin. Neither the children nor their parents knew what the children were eating. The parents kept records of their children's behavior.

The study found that "the children acted the same on either one of these sweeteners."

Final conclusion: there was no difference in either group's behavior.

What a shame!

Why not take one group of these children off all the chemical-filled junk and put them on natural, God-made foods such as fresh fruits and vegetables? Then there would surely be a difference.

Regrettably, individual families that I know of have already proven these findings. The parents in this study simply removed one bad thing from their children and replaced it with another.

It frustrates me to see these kinds of studies conducted, especially since you and I probably paid for that study with our hard-earned tax dollars. Now, no doubt, the families with hyperactive children will continue to let them eat all of the sugary foods they want, never knowing the real answer.

A Case of Misdiagnosis

My friend Ken told me of a time when he was twelve. He did not want to go to school and so told his Mother that he was sick. She let him stay home.

The next day he told her he was sick again. She let him stay home again. The third day he told her he was sick again.

She said, "Well, then, it is time to take you to the doctor." At the clinic, the doctor asked him, "Where does it hurt?" Ken stated, "Here," and pointed to his right side, exactly where the appendix was.

The doctor ran some extensive tests and afterwards announced, "This boy is having an appendicitis attack! We need to get him to a hospital immediately for surgery."

His mother was horrified and felt remorse for not taking her child to the doctor sooner. Of course, she consented, and he was rushed to the hospital for an appendectomy.

Thirty-five years later he was visiting his mother and announced, "Mom, remember when I had my appendix taken out? Well, I want to tell you I never had any pain on my side, and was never sick. I just did not want to go to school." Ken's mother was shocked. But no more shocked than that poor appendix!

When Ken's doctor examined that appendix, he undoubtedly knew it did not warrant removal, and probably knew that before, and when he made his diagnosis.

What a barbaric thing to do to a human being, especially a child!

Costly Colostomies

Indications are that the practice of surgical colostomies is more profitable than referring patients to colon hydrotherapists.

If a doctor cannot get a patient's colon to work properly after inundating it with drugs, laxatives, and an exam performed by a nurse, a colostomy is performed. In this surgery, the colon is surgically removed and replaced with a tube at the end of the small intestine. This tube is connected to a plastic bag worn outside the body.

The patient loses out under the knife, and spends the rest of his or her life with endless embarrassment as bags leak, stink, and often collapse during changing. In addition, complications can arise, and ongoing medical and prescription bills and wrangling with reluctant insurance companies provide a constant headache.

Not a pretty picture!

One colostomy recipient went for a job interview. Somehow, his bag broke and the stool spilled on the prospective employer's office floor. That applicant was so humiliated he went and committed suicide.

Someone very dear to me had a colostomy, and when I visited him I could hear the gas pass into his bag. He had no control over this. This was very humiliating to this honorable man.

How sad and yet unnecessary.

Contrasting this lengthy and costly procedure, internal cleansing improves the health of clients to the point where they actually do not need to visit the doctor.

CHAPTER FIVE

HOW YOUR BODY DIGESTS FOOD

Gary Lewkovich, D.C., tells of the experience of one of his patients whose constipation had advanced to a painful and debilitating stage:

We needed to clean out the severely impacted right side of her colon. In order to do so, it was imperative to get her on colon [hydrotherapy] right away.

For years, the patient had experienced abdominal pain, mood swings, indigestion, and an irritated ileocecal valve. She had twelve internal cleansing [sessions] before her symptoms were completely relieved. But soon into the [cleansing] program, she no longer had pain in the abdomen, her moods stabilized, and she was digesting properly.

A post X-ray showed that, sure enough, the valve had closed.

Initially we advised avoidance of certain foods. Because her ileocecal valve was so irritated, we could not start right away to increase her roughage intake. We had to get the valve closed first and then work on increasing the fiber in her diet.

After the ileocecal healed and began functioning properly, the patient's diet included greater amounts of fruits and vegetables to keep it healthy. These foods keep digesting matter as it moves along to the large intestine.

We have seen functional changes in the colon. Those changes include increased muscle tone. Without a doubt, internal cleansing is the answer for re-establishing the natural flow of the digestive system for many people, as this young woman's experience demonstrates.

Nutritious food, preferably organically grown, fuels your body. But this fuel has to be converted from large, more or less hard and dry pieces into something small - on the molecular level - soft, and moist before your body can use it.

The body performs this process of transformation using a combination of chemical and mechanical (muscular) actions to break down food. This process begins the moment you put food into your mouth, although your body usually prepares for digestion before this happens. Remember, the colon is a muscular organ.

When you think about, see, or smell food you like, especially if you are hungry, your mouth begins to water. This is saliva, a clear, tasteless liquid that resembles water but is actually a chemical produced by the salivary glands in your mouth. Saliva carries a digestive enzyme that breaks down starches into simple sugar and begins to digest your food.

Saliva mixes into the food you chew. The food is reduced to a soft, moist, bland little ball which, when it is ready to be swallowed, your tongue tosses to the back of your mouth where a reflexive muscle forces the food into your esophagus, beginning the downward muscular propulsion we call swallowing.

The large intestine has three parts: the ascending, transverse, and descending. The cecum, which rises sharply on the right side of the abdomen, is the beginning of the ascending colon. The large intestine becomes the transverse colon as it crosses over at the liver to the left side of the abdomen below the stomach. It becomes the descending colon as it plunges about six inches downward on the left side to where the sigmoid is (usually as far as an enema can get). The intestine forms a loop called the sigmoid flexure, which opens into the rectum.

The rectum ends in the anal canal, just above the anus, the opening to the outside of the body. The anus is normally closed tightly by two contracted sphincters. When you need to pass the waste products from a meal, you consciously relax the anal sphincters, allowing elimination of the feces.

By the time the chyme (partially digested food) reaches the cecum, your body tries to glean every usable molecule of fuel it can. So, instead of simply shooting through the colon, the chyme, becoming feces (or part waste material) makes a tortured trip through a succession of pouches.

Actual digestion is minimal in the colon. Because of harmful bacterial activity on the waste material, feces remaining here too long begin to poison the body. The kind of feces affected this way are usually not waste products from fruits, vegetables, grains, raw nuts, seeds, or legumes.

Bacteria naturally dwell in your colon: the "friendly" group (mainly lactobacillus acidophilus, bifidus), and the preferably much smaller colony of anaerobic bacteria (E. coli II). Malabsorption and illness can result from an imbalance or absence of these bacteria. The ideal ratio should be four to one - lactobacillus acidophilus to E. coli II. Unfortunately, the typical American diet reverses that balance, resulting in health problems. When doctors prescribe antibiotics, friendly bacteria are destroyed along with the harmful organisms, yet most M.D.'s fail to tell patients to replenish their bodies with lactobacillus acidophilus and bifidus the friendly bacteria.

Compared to the muscular activity of the previous parts of the digestive tract, the colon is less vigorous. But two or three times a day, if one is eating a healthy, high-fiber diet, a strong motion called a mass peristalsis is generally experienced, stimulated by the pressure of the fecal masses on the lower rectum, which first becomes distended with its load and then contracts against it.

The first of these peristalses is typically not noticed, but each succeeding mass peristaltic wave grows stronger until the need to go to the toilet to relieve that pressure becomes urgent.

Some people ignore or suppress these urges. Even if such a person eats a very healthful diet, this retention "discourages" the colon, which then tolerates the fecal mass and produces fewer and weaker peristalses. Suppression, may actually stop peristalsis altogether. If this happens, a person becomes constipated.

111

The longer feces sit in the colon, the more water is absorbed from them, making them dry and hard. As more fecal matter descends, it adds to that mass, making the feces larger - so large they may tear the anus when they finally, with much straining, get pushed out (this contributes to hemorrhoids, which are the result of excessive pressure on the tiny, delicate tissues and blood veins supplying the anal sphincters). This condition is also aggravated by an improper diet, low in vegetable matter, or fiber, and high in animal flesh, refined carbohydrates, highly processed, dairy products, and other refined foods, and by not drinking enough water.

That's why you need to heed nature's call from the beginning! The stuff sitting inside the body is stagnating, rotting, and resultant toxins are being reabsorbed into the body, killing the lactobacillus acidophilus and encouraging the E. coli II to proliferate wildly. These bacteria radically increase the toxins the colon is still absorbing.

Autointoxication

People are poisoning themselves from the inside out (known as autointoxication or autotoxemia). Brought on by a body desperately trying to defend itself against disease, this condition is an invitation to a weakened immune system for viral and bacterial attack, vulnerability to allergens, and hormonal and other chemical imbalances. The body will excrete offensive odors as it tries to eliminate accumulated sewage through pores and other body areas (like the mouth, ears, nose, groin, armpits, and vagina).

It is not an attractive state!

An Appreciative Wife's Story

A letter from a client's wife states:

My husband was a heavy meat and sweets eater who ate his biggest meal late at night. When he would come home from work his breath smelled like something had crawled into his body and died.

112

It was awful! He also had a potbelly but was thin everywhere else.

He did a nine-day juice fast monitored by Millan, herbal colon cleanses and colon hydrotherapy each day. She put him on a nutritious diet after his cleanse.

Now his breath is sweet smelling, no matter what time of the day, even in the morning when he awakes. His abdomen is now totally flat.

In a healthy individual, the total time for digestion from mouth to anus, varies four to twenty-six hours, depending on what is eaten. One should expect to have two to three bowel movements a day, usually after each meal.

A Client's Quick Relief

First, let me thank you for the quick relief you gave me in my time of need. As you know, I was backed up and did not have a bowel movement for a week. This was causing me sharp pain day and night. Every hour, I was walking the floor with pains in my abdomen.

I felt so bloated that I did not want to eat anymore. Not being able to have a bowel movement is very serious. Something had to be done about it.

My doctor recommended that I see you for several colon cleansing sessions. After the first session, I was able to sleep six hours straight without waking up. After the next few sessions, my bowel habits returned to normal!

I can eat and sleep again thanks to your internal cleansing!

Robert

Digestion in Herbivores/Carnivores

Human beings need plant matter in our diet.

If we compare the digestive tracts of herbivores to carnivores, we find that plant-eating animals tend to have rather long intestinal tracts, whereas flesh-eating animals have relatively short ones.

A carnivore's (meat-eating animal) short digestive tract suggests it was designed to reduce the time meat spends going through it. Logically, this also reduces the degree of putrefaction of fleshy waste products attained before elimination. Plant materials are easily digestible, so plant eaters have elaborate digestive systems to glean all possible nutrients from their diet.

Our human digestive tracts resemble those of herbivores - plant eating animals - (this gives a possible clue as to why people who eat a lot of vegetables and fruits, grains, legumes, and raw nuts and seeds have fewer bowel and health problems).

A vegetarian's food does not tend to putrefy.

However, meat rots in the digestive tract, spending more time going from mouth to anus, and, consequently, there are far greater opportunities for poisonous wastes to be introduced, absorbed and circulated in the bloodstream.

Parts of the Digestive System

The digestive system consists of the alimentary canal and accessory organs. The colon is a part of the alimentary canal, which has an oral cavity, pharynx, esophagus, stomach, small intestine, duodenum, jejunum, gall bladder and cystic duct, common bile duct, pancreas, and spleen.

The colon has two functions: to absorb water, sodium, and other minerals for the body's electrolyte supply, and to receive and reduce the chyme from the small intestine and store it for subsequent discharge.

Elimination

The brain senses the rectum's distension, and gives one the urge to have a bowel movement. Voluntary nerve impulses can inhibit the evacuation reflex, but this is a poor practice. Since the defecation reflex is weak, many voluntary muscles are called upon to assist the involuntary ones.

Colon X-rays

I recommend that my clients with lower digestive problems have an X-ray. A barium X-ray, sometimes called a lower G.I., will detect many problems including redundancy, spasticity, atony, ulceration, carcinoma and diverticulitis. One X-ray showed piles of calcium tablets lodged in a patient's ileocecal valve. The supplements were a total waste of time and money because there was no benefit, but irritation.

Upon examining the first X-ray, a patient should not be surprised to discover how twisted, looped, and possibly ballooned the colon looks. After a series of internal cleansing, another X-ray will reveal the amazing difference in the shape of the colon. It will look more normal than before.

Constipation test

A charcoal test may be taken to determine the degree of constipation.

If the bowels move at 8:00 a.m., charcoal (purchased at any health food store) is taken then and again at 4:00 p.m. the same day. If some of the charcoal is not passed by the second morning after it was taken, a person is regarded as constipated. The major portion of any one meal's residue should be expelled within forty-eight hours. Undue delay is failure to expel within a period of seventy-two hours.

Internal Cleansing and Intestinal Mucus

Removal of mucus is not an initial objective in internal cleansing. The colon walls normally secrete the substance, and during the session the mucus secretion increases as the contractions of the colon cause the mucus-secreting goblet cells to release mucus.

After healing or toxin removal the thickened mucus can be sloughed off.

Normal mucus coatings are not removed during the sessions.

Skin Brushing

It is very important to brush the skin while cleansing the body. A good skin brush can be bought at the health food store.

Because skin is the largest eliminator of toxins and poisons, you can be sure it is excreting a lot of these impurities. The only area to avoid brushing is the delicate skin of the face. There are special brushes available for this.

My clients skin brush daily on dry skin before bathing. All of the body, even the bottom of the feet, is brushed. With this daily routine, body skin feels refreshed and facial skin looks smoother and more radiant.

When I have a client with bad acne or pimples, I have found the greatest improvement on this condition is to daily skin brush all of the body, while cleansing. I have had people with severe acne tell me this, as in the following letter from Joseph:

Dear Millan,

It is just amazing to me to see that such a simple thing as internal cleansing, cleansing herbs, the special diet, and the skin brushing has improved the condition of acne I have suffered with.

I have been to many dermatologists and they gave me different prescriptions, but nothing has made such a difference as your cleansing program.

I do not feel embarrassed to look at people in the face with my new face. Thank you, again.

During this period of cleansings it is very important to skin brush daily on dry skin before bathing.

When the body is detoxifying, the skin is working to eliminate. Skin brushing expedites the cleanse.

CHAPTER SIX

AILMENTS OF THE DIGESTIVE SYSTEM AND THEIR CAUSES

Can you find your pet ailment, complaint, or medical condition among the following health problems?

Bad breath (despite proper oral hygiene); chronic skin dryness or blemishes; sallow skin; lifeless, dull hair (not due to chemical over-processing, such as bleaching, coloring or perming); psoriasis; and nail fungus.

Nail fungus, for example, is nearly impossible to heal. Patients serious about eradicating it completely, rather than spending money on endless preparations that do not work and the time and inevitable pain as the nail is eaten away, often submit to podiatrists who usually have no choice but to suggest removal of the nails.

But before taking that radical step, one patient, Richard, went the following route of internal cleansing:

I went to the podiatrist because I had fungus on my toenails. He initially told me it would take eight months for this fungus to clear up, and he only gave a sixty percent success rate if I had the toenails removed.

He wanted to give me a prescription, stating the drug did have side effects and it was very expensive, $2.50 a pill.

I refused and went the internal cleansing route. Shortly after, I started internal cleansing. I also changed my diet and took lactobacillus acidophilus and received lactobacillus acidophilus-bifidus implants at the end of my colon cleansing sessions.

I then went back to the doctor. He was amazed and stated that the progress I made in this month was remarkable.

Bob Completely Recovers

According to the following letter, another common ailment that has been effectively helped by internal cleansing is psoriasis. Bob's story, as told by his wife, reflects how internal cleansing helped him!

Bob, my husband, had psoriasis all over his body for years. His father, brother, and sister all had bad cases of it. Bob had inherited a genetic propensity for psoriasis.

We can inherit the weakness but we do not have to develop the actual disease!

Bob wore long pants and long sleeves when we would go to the islands and play golf. He never went to a pool, never went to the beach. He had to wear these long clothes.

It was horrible.

And he lived with it because he believed the doctors who had told him psoriasis was incurable.

I went everywhere to try to find a cure.

I could not believe nor accept anything less.

I just could not.

We went to a nutritional doctor. He told Bob to eat stir-fry and take vitamins, and then he was going to get well.

We believed him. But Bob's body was still covered with scabs.

For a year we searched. There were no answers. Then we went to the Holy Land, and when we came back my husband looked like he had leprosy. I was so scared. I could not believe it. That is the day something happened.

I said, "Let's pray before we do anything," and we did.

We always prayed before he left for work. He left for work, and this particular morning we thought he was dying.

I prayed that morning to God that something would happen.

I just felt like Bob was dying, and I was dying with him. I then remembered a woman I had met at a health lecture I gave on vitamins.

118

She had gone to a doctor, and he got her off all the drugs she was taking.

I heard her, but did not pay much attention because I was trying to present the lecture. So later, when I got back in the car, God began to speak to my heart.

An audible voice literally screamed at me, "Call Dr. _____!" who was the doctor this lady had recommended. Bob and I discussed it, and he decided to see the doctor.

The doctor said, "Do you want to get well? Do internal cleansing."

Internal cleansing was available at that office, so Bob began internal cleansing, then and there. We had no idea what was in store. Bob came home and began the dietary cleansing program. As far as we were concerned, if this was not going to benefit him, he was dead. There was no other answer.

Bob took one colon cleansing every day for six weeks and diligently ate nothing but raw vegetables, fruits, grains, nuts, beans, and legumes. He began to see the sores going away.

At the end of six weeks, Bob had no psoriasis.

Joanne

It has been over five years, now, and he does not have a sore on his body.

I should note here that a recovery like Bob's takes discipline, and not everyone achieves desired results. Even a seemingly unrelated condition such as psoriasis, which conventional medicine has no cure for, and is completely baffled by, has been helped by internal cleansing.

The List Gets Longer

Other symptoms of toxicity are unexplained weakness, fatigue, listlessness, lethargy, or sluggishness; inability to focus or concentrate, confusion, "spaciness," apathy, or depression; unexplained mood swings, irritability, or chronic, unexplained anxiety.

119

Abdominal pain, especially on the right side; weight that just will not come off, a persistent pot belly, uncontrollable food cravings, overeating without feeling satisfied, bloatedness, excess gas, or poor or increased appetite; coated tongue; unexplained recurrent nausea; pseudo-hypoglycemia; food sensitivities; asthma; chronic bronchitis or other respiratory problems; chronic cold or flu-like symptoms; sinusitis; common headaches or migraines; hypersensitivity to light, smoke, or perfume; and allergies.

My Daughter's Recovery From Allergies

My daughter Roxanne had terrible allergies and was taking those horrible shots to combat it. I kept telling her, "Honey, just clean out your body and change your diet and your allergies will go away."

She would say, "Oh, mother, it is not the food I eat, it is the pollen and cat hair I am allergic to."

So one night she came home (her husband and she were living with me at the time) and said she was going to go on a spiritual fast for five days because she had just become a born-again Christian and wanted to draw closer to Jesus. I immediately started giving her cleansing herbs and the second day she did internal colon cleansing. She was shocked to see what came out of her body. She continued with more colon cleansing sessions.

She never had the allergies again. Today, she herself is a very successful colon hydrotherapist.

You know our children, they never believe their mothers! She commented on how lovely her skin looked, because before she had slight blemishes around her chin area.

Back Pain and Other Common Ailments

Joint pain, gout, high blood pressure, atherosclerosis, and high cholesterol; those clients who have suffered from chronic sciatica, pain or numbness in lower extremities, or unexplained back pain all have experienced relief through internal cleansing.

Chronic back pain of mysterious origin plagues countless, otherwise healthy, people, often resulting in disability so severe they cannot do the simplest things or hold down jobs.

Even with diagnosable causes, doctors can do little, short of experimental surgery, to ease the pain. Many back surgeries are unsuccessful in achieving that aim.

Certainly a heavily impacted and poisonous colon contributes to the problem, as it puts pressure on the sciatic and lumbar nerves. But this aspect is almost universally overlooked by conventional physicians.

One of the symptoms of worms and parasites is a backache.

Chiropractors can make adjustments that can help. But, more important, internal cleansing, with the detoxification program, has helped many clients. The following is a letter from one such client:

I have a fifth lumbar vertebra which is cracked on one side and crushed on the other. For ten years I suffered mornings upon arising because of pressure on the fifth vertebra. When getting out of bed, I would have to walk for ten to fifteen minutes until the discomfort would go away.

I cannot explain it, but after doing internal cleansing sessions and the cleansing program, this pain in the back disappeared and I have not had it since.

Winnie

The Symptoms Keep Coming

For women, sometimes uncomfortable or even painful sexual intercourse; persistent unexplained vaginal odor; chronic or recurring yeast infections; and PMS are other symptoms.

If a person has or has had one or more of the following health problems, perhaps the state of the health of the colon should be seriously considered.

Practically all chronic, and most acute, physical and physiological ailments can be at least partially traced back to an unhealthy bowel. All these ailments can be adversely affected by a sick, clogged colon.

These problems could be gall bladder problems, liver problems not due to cirrhosis or hepatitis; tendencies toward nicotine, drug, alcohol, or caffeine addictions; basic immune deficiency (not the genetic condition or AIDS); chronic susceptibility to illness; hormonal imbalances. Indigestion, "nervous bowel," or irritable bowel syndrome; constipation, diarrhea, hemorrhoids, diverticulosis, or diverticulitis; frequent use of laxatives or products such as Kaopectate or Pepto-Bismol; offensive, persistent body odor, despite daily bathing and hygiene.

There is more; get the picture?

A Case of Restored Fertility

Believe it or not, evidently even some conditions of infertility can be an effect of an unhealthy colon, as Sherry, a client, illustrates:

For five years my husband and I tried very hard to have a baby but could not. I was artificially inseminated many times. I developed a cyst in the ovaries from the side effects of the medication I had to take.

Finally, my husband and I had internal cleansing in a series of ten colon cleansings for each of us.

We also followed the cleansing program Millan recommended.

One month after we completed our series, I got pregnant.

I honestly believe cleansing our bodies and strengthening our immune systems had something to do with my getting pregnant.

Since going through the cleansing program, my cyst is gone and we now have a beautiful healthy baby boy!

Addiction

It makes sense that an inefficient digestive system would encourage addictions. When the colon is clogged with rotting garbage, it cannot get rid of toxins. In fact, these poisons get reabsorbed into the body. In turn, the body, under attack by poisons and out of balance, seeks ways of hastening absorption, and the brain seeks chemical relief.

Clients stated that internal cleansing and detoxification have alleviated their toxic conditions by enabling the body to kick addictive habits.

Addiction is a process of habituation over a period of weeks, months, or, more often, years.

Withdrawal is difficult and usually painful, both psychologically and physically. Rehabilitation programs often do not work because this transition to non-addiction is so painful, including violent fevers, sweating, weakness with muscular contractions and uncontrollable trembling, nausea, and diarrhea.

These excruciating and humiliating symptoms last anywhere from a few hours to a few days, and the residual psychological craving can hang on for torturous years. Counseling and support groups are nice, but are too often inadequate for the addict's ultimate success.

Internal cleansing, with a detoxification program, should be considered as a definite means to break the addiction.

During the body's natural cleansing process, all foreign matter is sent to the liver for detoxification. From there it is delivered to the excretory organs, the kidneys and the digestive tract via bile, for elimination from the body.

A slow-moving, unhealthy colon causes reabsorption of the drug-laden bile. To break the reabsorption cycle, the waste products stored in the large bowel must be evacuated.

A detoxification cleansing program and internal cleansing performs just this function, with the added benefit that it stimulates a sluggish colon to begin normal peristalsis. Internal cleansing can assist in an efficient, gentle way to help the addict defeat addiction. I believe internal cleansing should be a required step in any drug rehabilitation program.

Even years later, the effects of drug use can be purged from the body. One client commented that

123

she had smoked pot regularly for a short period in her youth, but that she had not partaken for ten years.

She went through a cleansing program of a juice fast, internal cleansing sessions and herbal cleansers. On this regimen, she experienced a mild high, as if she were stoned on pot.

It could be that the THC, or tetrahydrocannabinol, was stored in her fat cells and other tissues for many years, and started releasing into the bloodstream and being eliminated out of her body.

Another client who had been a heroin addict said she had not used heroin for fifteen years. When she did a cleansing program with internal cleansing, she said she could actually smell the unique odor of the heroin seep out of the pores of her skin.

Medical studies have shown that certain insoluble chemicals can indeed be stored in fat cells and other tissues, sometimes to deadly effect, as with DDT.

Even over-the-counter drugs can build up toxins in the body and may lead to dependence on the substance. When this happens, internal cleansing can bring the relief needed. Here is the case of one man's experience with nasal spray:

I was taking nasal spray for twenty-four years. I was doing up to one twelve-hour bottle a week, spraying every two hours. I could never get off it without having severe side effects, such as nasal swelling, fever, throat swelling, and basic inability to breathe.

While doing the colon cleansing program and after my second internal cleansing session, I went off the spray. I have had absolutely no problems and have been off it ever since.

Robert

Another client, a former alcoholic who was sober for twelve years, had a series of internal cleansing sessions coupled with the dietary and herbal cleansing programs. Soon after, his body began to reek of stale booze. The odor eventually went away as all the garbage was finally eliminated from his body.

But the process was quite an experience! The Dotolo Institute states the following:

Recent observations proved that internal cleansing is very beneficial as part of a drug rehabilitation program, insofar as test persons indicated a considerable reduction in the craving for addictive drugs. A closely controlled test series in drug-rehabilitation centers is being prepared at present.

Internal Cleansing
and Substance Rehabilitation

Internal cleansing facilitates drug rehabilitation by eliminating the drugs and their toxic byproducts, minimizing painful and harrowing withdrawal symptoms, and should be part of all drug detoxification programs.

Opium derivatives (heroin, morphine, etc.) actually decrease bowel activity, and cocaine and its myriad derivatives are absorbed at a much higher rate than the liver can filter out; therefore, internal cleansing is a critical necessity for drug addicts.

Even addicts to nicotine, caffeine, and alcohol get the same benefits from colon cleansing as hard drug users; in light of this, if they want to stop smoking or drinking with relatively minimal trauma, these habitual users should complete a program of detoxification with internal cleansing.

Doctors Discuss Autotoxemia

Fifty-seven prominent British physicians met in London to discuss the problem of autointoxication (or autotoxemia).

These eminent doctors determined the major cause of autotoxemia to be an inefficient, "toxic" colon.

They identified twenty-two poisons as originating from an unhealthy colon. Among them are a chilling array of lethal toxins, including cadaverine, cresol, botulin, putrescine, ammonia, methylmercaptam, methylgardinine, sulfuroglov-

125

bine, sulfuretted hydrogen, or hydrogen sulfide, sepsis, hydrogen, indole, phenol, nitric acid, urobilin, histidine, muscarine, indican, neurin, ptomaine, pentemethylendiamine, and indoethylamine.

These toxic chemicals also kill the genuinely beneficial micro-organisms - lactobacillus acidophilus and bifidus bacteria - enabling the marginally beneficial smaller colony of E. coli II to thrive and multiply out of control, spewing ever more deadly poisons into our bloodstream and tissues.

Is it any wonder, then, that our bodies get sick, and in all possible ways?

What is toxic in its raw form outside our bodies does not change its toxic effects when cycled throughout our bodies. We allow our colon to become clogged with toxins through poor diet and lifestyle, bad toilet training, medical and scientific ignorance, and culturally mandated indifference.

Many poisons stay in our bodies for a lifetime. This toxicity causes illness and a rundown immune system. I believe that autointoxication, left untreated, ages us.

Jaw and Dental Ailments

Some forms of TMJ (temporomandibular joint syndrome) are particularly mysterious and unbearably painful to its sufferers. Clients with this condition have stated that a thorough body cleansing through internal cleansing and dietary cleansing have helped to control inflammation of the jaw area.

Other forms of oral maladies have been responsive to internal cleansing, as this case indicates:

For a year I suffered an extremely painful condition that made sores in my mouth. The pain was constant and so great that my whole jawbone area swelled visibly. I took aspirin regularly, but it did not help. My dentist recommended I see a specialist, since nothing he tried worked.

But the specialist could not help me, either. All he recommended was surgery, and warned me I might have cancer.

126

Desperate, I tried internal cleansing. After a few sessions, to my relief, the pain went away completely, and I have had the first pain-free week in over a year.

Recently I went back to my doctor and told him of my experience with internal cleansing.

He said, "What's that?"

I am glad I know what it is, and thanks to it, all the anticipation of possible surgery and fear of cancer is now behind me.

I am very grateful.

Walter

Diabetes

Several experiences with diabetics seem to point to internal cleansing programs as a way to lessen the effects of the disease. Diabetics have claimed victory over the devastating consequences of this often progressively debilitating disease, which can lead to blindness, kidney failure, gangrene with amputation of feet and legs, and, of course, premature death.

If the true aim of medicine is to alleviate as much undue suffering as possible when an absolute cure may not be attainable, then the response of diabetic conditions to internal cleansing should be looked at closely by the medical community.

This story from Charles highlights the point:

Before internal cleansing, I was diagnosed with Type II diabetes. My blood sugar level averaged 150 to 180 every morning. Sometimes it went as high as 300 when I ate donuts.

But I found out that these levels were dangerous.

I started internal cleansing, with the internal cleansing program.

After the sixth colon cleansing session, my blood sugar level dropped to an average of 100 and then became normal, even though during my series I blew it twice by eating donuts! I tested my blood level when I did this and it had not gone up!

I tried to believe that I was cured of diabetes, but I know I was not. I know I must watch my diet.

Doctors tell diabetics to watch their diets, but that is easier said then done. It is like telling a drug addict not to do drugs. I know how much the internal cleansing helped keep my cravings for sugar down.

Internal cleansing has made all the difference in my eating habits, especially my cravings. Overall, my energy has increased and I feel great.

It is perfectly logical that what goes into your body must affect it, otherwise we would not need to eat, period. Because this is not a perfect world, we live in intimate contact with harmful micro-organisms and potentially toxic chemicals - many of which are made and given off even by otherwise benign microorganisms.

This happens in our own digestive system.

Respiratory Disease

The process of digestion requires the cooperation of microorganisms living in our bowels, and without which we cannot live. We depend on these tiny creatures to digest our food and release its nutrients into our bloodstream.

The aorta, the large artery leading directly from the heart, picks up nutrients from the intestine and distributes them to all parts of the body. Since one of its vital distribution points is the lungs, respiratory disease should be linked to digestion more often than not.

Chronic bronchitis, a common ailment of the respiratory system, is a response to environmental and internal toxins. When medical treatments, focusing on symptoms, cannot clear it up, it is logical to look for causes from within the body itself. The supply post for toxins is the colon.

Fermenting, decaying waste material is sent out into the bloodstream by the out-of-control E. coli II, which have taken over the clogged colon. Wide-ranging results follow, as the case of Frank clearly shows:

In the spring of 1983 I developed bronchitis. By November I was at my wit's end because nothing I did made it any better.

When I read that an impacted colon blocks the normal elimination systems of the body, causing a backup of toxins to the organs, I questioned if it applied to my situation.

The article highlighted the mucus deposits in the lungs as a breeding ground for bacteria and resulting respiratory problems.

I decided to try a colon-cleansing series. Within two days the bronchitis disappeared.

The health benefits I have gained from bi-annual internal cleansing treatments have been beyond my greatest expectations. As my organs regained their health, the puffiness, lines, and other indications of advancing age lessened. My energy and stamina increased each year. My mental awareness and creativity are noticeably stronger after a series of internal cleansings.

Internal cleansing has also been a source of emotional release. Every emotional experience causes a chemical response in the body. Those chemicals are stored in the tissues when they cannot be effectively eliminated and are toxic to those tissues. Besides storing toxins, the tissues are typically deficient in necessary minerals because the walls of an impacted colon are unable to absorb them.

The bottom line of internal cleansing is that it eliminates all the accumulated toxins and allows proper absorption and distribution of the vital minerals to all the tissues. Another important benefit of internal cleansing is hydration, as most people are dehydrated. Some feel that is the number one benefit. People can get dizzy, though, with too much hydration.

Acne

And finally, for you sufferers of that scourge of young skin, let us discuss acne. A young lady in her mid-twenties came to me for internal cleansing. Her intent was to get rid of a bad case of pimples.

Her boyfriend had heard about internal cleansing and suggested she try it.

She did a series of ten internal cleansing sessions. By her sixth session, she started to see her skin clear up. When she came in for her seventh session she was ecstatic. She looked lovely, and her boyfriend was so happy at how nice she looked.

By the time she completed her series, her skin was totally cleared up.

Her unnecessary misery had been contributed to by a simple cause: a malfunctioning colon which began to poison her body and betrayed itself in her skin. She also had a history of previous drug abuse.

Autotoxemia: Researchers' Findings

The concept of autotoxemia was first articulated late in the last century by the eminent Russian bacteriologist, Metchnikoff. At the time, his discoveries were revolutionary because of their newness and far-ranging implications.

This was an age that was just beginning to see through more powerful and accurate microscopes the reality of bacteria and understand their prevalence and significance in the world.

The implications Metchnikoff theorized for these microorganisms were largely ignored in the United States. Yet, they influenced four generations of European physicians as far as bowel functions and overall health are concerned.

Metchnikoff believed that autotoxemia (self-poisoning) through putrefaction of metabolic wastes in the large intestine is the main cause of preventable illness and premature aging.

Recently Drs. Leo Galland, Senior Research Consultant of the Great Smokies Diagnostic Laboratory in Ashville, North Carolina, and Stephen Barrie, its president, released their findings on autotoxemia in a paper called "Intestinal Dysbiosis and the Causes of Disease."

In this report, these doctors bring Metchnikoff's research and theories into the twentieth century. While Metchnikoff studied the beneficial relationships between intestinal flora and the body, a state of "eu-symbiosis," he also "popularized the idea of dyssymbiosis, or dysbiosis, a state of living with intestinal flora that has harmful effects."

Yet, it is only in the last two decades, with the frightening rise in colo-rectal cancer, that Metchnikoff's ideas have been taken seriously here in the United States. Finally, serious research has begun on the relationship between our health - with emphasis on the colon - and what we eat.

Galland and Barrie's research "has implicated bacterial dysbiosis in a number of inflammations within the bowel or involving skin or connective tissue," such as atopic eczema, irritable bowel syndrome, and inflammatory bowel disease. The researchers further note the following:

Immunologic responses to gut flora have been advanced by several authors as important factors in the pathogenesis of inflammatory joint diseases. It is well-known that reactive arthritis can be activated by intestinal infections with... enterobacteria... Increased intestinal permeability and immune responses to bacterial debris may cause other types of inflammatory joint disease as well.

The researchers at the Great Smokies Laboratory found that "most adverse effects of the indigenous gut flora are caused by the intense metabolic activity" of bacteria mainly concerned with the waste products of food.

They continue:

The enzymes urease, found [in these organisms] and induced in [them] by a diet high in meat, hydrolyses [or transforms] urea to ammonia, raising stool pH. A relatively high stool pH is associated with a higher prevalence of colon cancer.

131

Conversely, the researchers state, "a relatively low stool pH is associated with protection against colon cancer."

They also found that "bacterial tryptophanase degrades tryptophan to carcinogenic phenols, and, like urease, is induced by a high-meat diet." An American diet, typically high in meat, is the major culprit in colo-rectal cancer. It is also receiving attention for contributing to breast cancer.

Galland and Barrie have more to say on the dangers of cancer-causing toxins in a clogged colon.

Bile acids irritate the colon's delicate lining and cause diarrhea. Moreover, bile acids "or their metabolites [byproducts] appear to be carcinogenic and are thought to contribute to the development of colon cancer, and to ulcerative colitis."

To further complicate a dangerous situation, gut bacteria are more likely to contribute to colon carcinogenesis (beginnings of cancer conditions in cells, or protocancers); in fact, the prevalence of colon cancer is proportional to stool concentration of [a particulate secondary bile acid]."

The researchers go on to state that these disturbances are caused by the high-fat, flesh and depleted fiber content which characterize Western diets and are consistent with Metchnikoff's theories.

The doctors' clinical assessment is the following: intestinal dysbiosis should be considered as a mechanism promoting disease in all patients with chronic gastrointestinal, inflammatory or autoimmune disorders, food allergy and intolerance, breast and colon cancer, and unexplained fatigue, malnutrition or neuropsychiatric symptoms.

One obvious answer to eliminating and preventing such disorders is initial internal cleansing along with diet correction.

Leslie Williams, former President of I.A.C.T., told me a study was done recently regarding internal cleansing. Ten participants that qualified had to go four days without a bowel movement.

Stool samples were taken to determine friendly flora content. As expected, many had none or very little. They received nine internal cleansing sessions each, for one month. During that time, they were not allowed to take lactobacillus acidophilus or yogurt. After the 30 days they took another stool sample. What they discovered was that their bacteria balance improved dramatically. The number one benefit they discovered also, was the hydration improvement allowing the mucus to flow more freely in the body. This is a very impressive discovery as to the benefits of internal cleansing.

Allergy Relief Story

In this successful case, the claim was made that life-long, serious allergies were relieved through internal cleansing and a detoxification cleansing program.

This is Mark's R.'s story:

For almost all of my life I have been an allergy/asthma sufferer, slobbering my way through college and career.

As if that was not enough, by the time I turned eighteen, I had developed symptoms of candidiasis, including constant fatigue, constipation, bloating, and the feeling that I was never quite digesting my food. Other symptoms included a new case of food allergies and exaggerated allergies to the environment, plus a numbing case of "brain fog," where I was unable to concentrate on any given task of the moment.

For the next twelve years I went from doctor to doctor, seeking relief from all of these symptoms. In return for such professional medical consultations, I received everything from treadmill tests and blood tests to the latest topical nasal and asthma sprays.

Of course, when the doctors discovered that the tests showed nothing and the drugs were not effective, the next role for the doctors to play was psychiatrist.

They fired at me questions like, "Are you happy with your job?" and "How often do you have sex?"

With that kind of medical attention, my future looked bleak. Fortunately, I was able to find one allergist who got me started on allergy shots and a rotational diet. The diet was excellent because it eliminated flour and dairy products.

I was finally getting some allergy relief.

Several months after starting the allergy shots, my nasal passages had still not cleared enough for easy breathing (You run a great health risk being a mouth breather all of your life. You never know what insect you may inhale!).

So, the same doctor kept pushing me to have surgery to correct a mildly deviated septum and my inflamed nasal membranes. I was convinced of the benefit and decided to go ahead with the surgery.

The results? A big fat NOTHING!

At least the shots and diet proved useful, but to a point that was short of the mark. I wanted more, and I wanted it right away.

I consulted acupuncturists, chiropractors, and colon hydrotherapists. I opted to go ahead with internal cleansing because it seemed to be the most hopeful of my options in getting rid of candidiasis.

After my second session, feeling very light on my feet, I went for a jog in the neighborhood, running the course that I always do. I was delighted to discover that I did not have to stop midstream to catch my breath. I had energy to spare! What's more, I ran home with no asthma attack, which was something new.

Some time after my third session, I was beginning to learn from personal experience the relationship between a clean, functioning colon and clear nasal passages.

It seems that clear breathing is proportional to the proper movement of the colon.

What an incredible discovery! I wonder how many other allergy problems that people have are related to this concept.

Too bad I wasted so much money on nasal surgery that did not help in the least. I am bothered every time I think of the doctor who was so sure that his surgery would work. He is missing a good part of the complete picture of good health.

By the end of the fourth session, I noticed a mood swing. My body was screaming "HAPPY," whether or not I wanted to be.

After the fifth session, I no longer had asthmatic reactions to foods, and my "brain fog" was lifting.

This is where I am so far in the program to better health. I am following Millan's recommended "cleansing" program before each session, and with each visit I have some new health achievement to report. Not only are the symptoms of candidiasis disappearing, the allergies and asthma problems are leaving as well.

Spring is typically the worst allergy season, but this spring has been the best I have ever had in my life. I believe my "slobbering" allergy days are becoming a thing of the past!

Thank you, Millan, for your patience, wisdom, and personalized care.

The only regret I have is that I did not start my recovery program with internal cleansing in the first place.

Constipation

The colon itself can suffer acute or chronic conditions. Probably the most familiar to all of us is constipation. This is often the first telltale sign of bad eating habits; however, the cause is blatantly overlooked because our American culture takes for granted harmful dietary intake.

In short, constipation, derived from a Latin word meaning to press, crowd together, pack, or cram, is exactly that - a colon packed with old drying fecal matter it has not been allowed to or cannot evacuate.

Constipation is caused directly by these things: an unhealthy diet consisting of too much meat, dairy products, cooked and processed foods; bad elimination habits and posture; drinking too little water; high stress levels, especially for women; illegal drugs and legal, over-the-counter or prescription medications; laxatives; lack of proper balance of vital intestinal bacteria; lack of exercise; cultural stigma in certain situations; and weakness of the abdominal muscles that aid evacuation. Other causes are low thyroid, gall bladder problems, and a dysfunctional liver.

Constipation can easily be understood to be a leading cause of disease and disease susceptibility. As previously stated, the longer rotting waste material stays in the body, the more toxins are produced. More tissues are broken down by toxic action which either store or excrete the toxins.

The body's defenses weaken as its arsenal is concentrated on internal adversaries rather than elements invading from the outside. Constipation reduces the body to this state, acting as an open invitation for disease - including colo-rectal cancer.

I tell my clients that if they think they are not constipated because they may have one or two bowel movements a day, "Think again!" I tell them, "If your diet is unhealthy, no matter how often you defecate, you may still have an impacted colon. Your colon may have waste matter trapped in excess mucus - produced by your desperate intestine which tries to trap and therefore neutralize all the bad stuff."

Waste products become impacted in the pockets of the colon, especially in the diverticula (those little pouches that hang like baggy growths on the walls of the colon). As more and more fecal matter becomes trapped, the center tunnel, where a limited amount of waste is allowed to pass, becomes more and more distorted, resulting in restrictive passage flow, even though elimination may occur twice a day.

In his book, *Become Younger*, Dr. Walker tells how in an autopsy he saw a colon which measured eleven inches in diameter, with a central passageway in the encrusted fecal matter of only the diameter of a pencil.

There is another danger in the mucoid fecal matter that builds up in an unhealthy colon: it provides a perfect breeding ground for harmful bacteria, and is a reservoir for all the harmful toxins the bacteria produce. Importantly, it is a pathway of disease agents resulting from poisons and free radicals. Opsudo memberiouses is a false membrane, formed as a response to too many antibiotics, which interferes with normal bowel flora and function.

Gary N. Lewkovich, D.C., cites eight reasons individuals develop constipation:

1. *Too little fiber in the diet.*
2. *Too little water consumed.*
3. *Too little exercise.*
4. *Too much stress.*
5. *Poor elimination habits.*
6. *Certain medications.*
7. *Certain foods.*
8. *Certain pathologies affecting the lower digestive tract.*

You cannot afford a clogged colon. Constipation is a serious condition that demands immediate attention if you desire good health. This leads to clogged conditions in other vital digestive systems as well. Your colon hydrotherapist can provide the path to good health.

Rich Anderson, author of *Cleanse and Purify Thyself*, himself went through a number of fasts and colon cleansings. He became amazed with the long strands of ropy mucoidal matter he saw coming out of him in the view-tube during internal cleansing.

Anderson attempted to categorize the consistent shapes and sizes of the mucoid fecal matter, based on the theory that the shapes of the pieces would indicate their origin in the intestine, in the same way that Play-Doh conforms to impressions. He thought that he could identify the sections of colon to which the slimy goo had been molded. The duration of colon impaction might be determined by the distance into the intestine. He states:

> If your colon has been impacted for some time, the body's natural defense against all the junk is to produce mucus to try to help trap it and move it out.
>
> The small intestine may become involved in producing this excess mucus. When that happens, the bile ducts may become blocked. Anderson states that if that happens, the essential bile fluids produced by the liver will not be able to reach the food for proper digestion and assimilation.

Bacterial and chemical chaos will ensue, with dire results as outlined in the previous discussion. Thus, the stage is set for all kinds of malfunctions and diseases, including precancerous and cancerous.

The Problem of Gas

Many factors contribute to the problem of gas, but, according to Dr. Gary Lewkovich, "Gas is most often a sign of one or more flaws in the complex process of digestion, absorption or elimination." He suggests the following to reduce occurrence of gas:

> 1. Do NOT eat quickly. Avoid stress while eating.
> 2. Chew your food thoroughly before swallowing.
> 3. Do NOT overeat.
> 4. Do NOT eat within two hours of bedtime.
> 5. Do NOT drink more than eight ounces of liquid with a meal.
> 6. Drink at least eight to ten glasses of pure water each day.
> 7. Eat your vegetables lightly steamed.
> 8. Avoid swallowing air as you chew or drink.
> 9. Avoid those foods that you have difficulty digesting.

10. *Minimize sweets (cookies, candies, syrups, etc.).*
11. *Minimize fatty or fried foods.*
12. *Minimize alcohol, coffee, and carbonated beverages.*
13. *Keep your meals simple, but vary them from day to day.*
14. *When using nutritional supplements, try to use the capsule or powder form, in preference to pills or tablets.*
15.*Exercise daily, but wait at least one hour after your meals to do so.*
16.*Eat when hungry, not according to the clock.*
17.*Use acidophilus - when indicated - to restore friendly colon bacteria.*
18.*Use digestive enzymes - when indicated - to help digestion of protein, fats and carbohydrates.*
19.*Use hydrochloric acid supplements - when indicated - to aid the digestion of proteins. Do NOT use it if you have an ulcer.*
20.*Keep your colon clean and healthy. Eat adequate amounts of appropriate high fiber foods but avoid laxatives.*

* *Please consult with the doctor before using any suggestion with an *.*

Cholesterol

Dr. William Welles, author of *The Shocking Truth About Cholesterol,* also asserts that the bile routes must remain unclogged because bile regulates cholesterol:

Cholesterol levels can actually be regulated by the body itself through the liver, provided that bile has a chance to act on fat. When bile breaks down fat the liver can then convert excess cholesterol into bile for future use.

When you ingest fat, the gall bladder contracts, releasing bile for digestion.

According to Welles, the bile is then reabsorbed further down the digestive tract.

If the colon is constipated, still more bile reabsorption takes place. The liver is signaled to produce less bile, with the consequence that less cholesterol is converted to bile and more is dangerously released into the bloodstream.

This indicates that often high cholesterol is less related to how much fat you eat but more to how well your colon is working; in other words, how much bile your liver can produce by cholesterol conversion.

Lymph System

Another vital body system affected directly by digestion is the lymph system. It has its own circulatory system and performs some of the same functions the blood does, like carrying away waste products from cells.

Nutrition counselor and author of *The Colon Health Handbook*, Robert Gray, believes that the colon is the principal organ into which the lymph deposits its wastes. Gray further theorizes that the colon has a special ability to detoxify lymph.

This cannot be accomplished, obviously, if there is an accumulation of putrefying fecal matter in the colon. So, like the colon, the lymphatic system can contain stagnant waste material.

If you clog the colon - a detoxifier and portal for lymph - you also clog the lymph system, and the toxins are redistributed throughout the body, contributing to its poisoning.

The importance of a well-functioning, properly moving colon cannot be overemphasized. You ignore it or mistreat it at your peril.

There are five channels of elimination in the body:
Skin
Colon
Lymph
Kidneys
Lungs

Hemorrhoids

Before we move on, one more direct result of constipation must be addressed. This is hemorrhoids. Hemorrhoids, or piles, are not caused by reading on the toilet. Hemorrhoids are caused by straining at the toilet to eliminate during constipation. It is common to see them in internal cleansing.

The pressure, both from the obvious weight and bulk of the accumulated feces and from muscles striving to push the hardened matter out, also pushes out, literally inverting, the inner lining and tissues of the anal sphincters.

The constriction is so severe on the delicate tissues and their capillaries that it ruptures many of them, causing localized internal - and sometimes external - bleeding, an obvious invitation for infection. It produces what are essentially varicose veins in the anus.

"Piles" are the pockets of blood and damaged tissues that make up hemorrhoids. They often protrude outside the anus when having a bowel movement. As you may know, this condition is extremely painful. The huge amounts of Preparation H and such remedies and the brisk sales of "tush cushions" testifies to its prevalence.

I tell my clients this condition could be avoided by simply taking proper care of their colon through diet and cleansing.

Thanks to our cultural attitude toward the bowels, it is little known or acknowledged that straining at the toilet is also a leading cause of sudden death and fatal heart attack among the elderly. Many collapse and die right on the toilet.

Out of "respect for the dead," we just do not talk about this as a cause of death; it is a "shameful," certainly unnecessary, death in our culture.

Laxatives

Wow! Better rush right to the medicine cabinet and start chugging down those laxatives, right? Wrong! Frequent use of laxatives, even the "bulking" ones, actually contributes to constipation, the very condition it purports to eliminate.

Most laxatives work by chemically poisoning and irritating the lining of the colon, the very tissue and muscle that channels nutrients and wastes from the bloodstream. Naturally, the irritated colon heaves in super-agitated contractions in a desperate attempt to get rid of the offending laxatives. Anything loose enough to flow out with the resulting diarrhea will be expelled.

This emergency rush of watery stool is really massive dehydration. Dehydration of the colon produces constipation. So, the vicious cycle continues, with the consequent need for possibly another stronger laxative dose.

Several things happen: the chronically constipated colon comes to depend on the irritant stimulus of the laxative to contract for defecation. This causes a dependence on the laxative, the laxative causes dehydration, dehydration causes constipation, and dependence on laxatives causes the colon to become ever more weakened. Even herbal laxatives can cause the colon to become dependent on them.

A typical, lifelong American diet, combined with various medications, causes an aging bowel to get tired and just give up. Many chronic sufferers of constipation are middle-aged or elderly.

The real beneficiaries of laxatives are those who make and sell them. The financial success of these companies and their distributors is clear evidence that we Westerners are having a collective colon crisis; therefore, it is clear that internal cleansing, which contributes to good health, is vitally needed and should be implemented.

Diarrhea

Diarrhea refers to bowel movements that occur too often and are too loose. Diarrhea can be caused by impacted fecal matter, viruses, an acute imbalance of intestinal bacteria, unfamiliar foods and food intolerance, allergies, attacks of external bacteria (such as cholera, typhoid, or bacillary dysentery), eating unripe fruit or tainted food or water, emotional turmoil (such as fear, nervousness, or rage), or infestation of parasites such as worms or amoebas (as in amoebic dysentery).

Diarrhea may even be a symptom of cancer. If the stools are black or there is blood in them, one should immediately seek a doctor.

People suffer from diarrhea quite frequently in our culture. There are many reasons people get diarrhea, but the most common is constipation.

So many times, clients complain of constipation, then diarrhea, then again constipation, followed by diarrhea.

What happens is the colon has so much impaction that the colon muscles cannot expel the feces. The body senses this irritation in attempts to remove the impaction. It washes it with fluid, causing diarrhea which is the liquid form that expels out of the colon. As a result, stool becomes hard as a rock, tearing delicate tissues and creating a hemorrhoid.

Irritable Bowel Syndrome

Gastroenterologists cite irritable bowel syndrome as the most common aliment. Symptoms of this frustrating and painful condition are abdominal pain (only temporarily relieved by frequent bowel movements), a bloated or distended abdomen, and mucus in the stools. Rectal bleeding is not a trademark of this condition.

Irritable bowel syndrome is brought on by a variety of causes, including nervousness and anxiety, unfamiliar food, too spicy food, food allergies and intolerance, and, of course, bad diet.

Inflammatory Bowel Disease

Resembling irritable bowel syndrome is inflammatory bowel disease. But the latter's cause is a serious imbalance of intestinal flora. The toxins given off by suddenly proliferating "bad bacteria" irritate and inflame the lining of the bowel and may cause ulceration or perforation of the delicate colon wall.

Obviously, an impacted, constipated colon can be deadly in this case. Unhealthy diet and a stagnating colon are to blame.

This disease continues to subvert conventional views of the importance of diet in the colon and overall health. A more complete discussion of this condition can be found in Galland's and Barrie's report, "Intestinal Dysbiosis and the Causes of Disease," cited above and available from the Great Smokies Diagnostic Laboratory in Asheville, North Carolina.

Ulcerative Colitis

Ulcerative colitis is an inflammation of the lining of the colon, with possible complications due to perforation of the wall. Again, it is the product of bad diet, improper colon function, and bowel habits.

Crohn's Disease

Crohn's disease is a different kind of inflammation that can occur anywhere in the digestive tract from the mouth to the rectum, but characteristically it is found in the lower bowel. The inflammation attacks the entire wall of the colon, not just its interior lining.

Dr. Henry Janowitz has noted that people who suffer from these inflammatory diseases have depressed immune systems. He suspects that the decreased immune response may be a direct result of the disease and not the cause.

Diverticulosis/Diverticulitis

Diverticulosis is a condition in which abnormal diverticula (sac-like pouches), develop on the walls of the digestive tract. Most are found on the colon.

This condition is caused by impacted fecal matter. When the pouches become inflamed, the condition is known as diverticulitis. The irritation can be severe, in some cases perforating the colon, necessitating surgery.

The constant irritation and drain on the immune system is an invitation to cancer.

This condition is more common in civilized society, with high-meat, low-fiber diets. It is especially dangerous in the elderly. It is well documented that the lowest incidents of diverticulotsis in our society is among the Seventh-Day Adventists, due to their life style, including a low intake of meat and high intake of fruits, vegetables, and grains.

Candidiasis

Candidiasis is a relatively newly recognized bowel ailment. Its symptoms are varied and often confused with other maladies. Too often, misinformed doctors dismiss the symptoms as psychosomatic - all in the head of the sufferer.

Candidiasis comes from the Latin word "candida." It is an opportunistic yeast that proliferates in the body when "good" bacteria are absent. It produces toxins along with the overpopulating "bad" bacteria, with consequent ill effects on the body.

Parasites and Worms

Parasites and worms are another largely overlooked health threat in the United States. Dr. Zane Gard, M.D., and other doctors estimate that approximately eighty to ninety percent of our population unknowingly harbors worms and parasites of one sort or another.

Worms are given the opportunity to invade the body through bad hygiene. Amoebas may ulcerate the walls of the colon and invade the circulatory system, where they are distributed everywhere in the body.

People can contract parasites and worms through water, even distilled water, air, foods such as meats, fish, chicken, fruits, vegetables, even organic vegetables, pets and other people.

A Flu Victim's Story of Recovered Health

When I first called Rainbow Nutrition, a four-week-old flu was still hanging on. I was experiencing pre-menopausal night sweats, and I was about twenty pounds overweight.

Millan addressed all my questions and suggested I come out later that afternoon and give internal cleansing a try.

I could hardly believe it when the very next morning all signs of my flu were gone.

I started on the detoxification program and a series of the internal cleansing sessions, taking one every week. Within a period of three months, I had lost the twenty pounds and cleaned enough toxins from my body so that the night sweats had ceased. My skin looked clearer and my energy level increased.

My own experience has taught me that internal cleansing and correct eating are the two most important factors in regaining youth and health.

Sandra

Colo-rectal Cancer

Finally, the most dreaded and devastating of possible colon ailments: colo-rectal cancer.

In the alimentary canal the most common cancers are stomach cancer and colo-rectal cancer. The latter disease is almost exclusively a phenomenon of the Western world, with the highest incidence reported in the United States. It is now recognized that colo-rectal cancer is directly linked to a high-meat, low-fiber diet.

Colo-rectal cancer is usually found either in the ileocecal area at the beginning of the colon, or at the site of the sigmoid and rectum; hence, the compound name of the disease, colo-rectal.

This fatal disease claims the lives of over sixty thousand people annually.

CHAPTER SEVEN

THE SOLUTION TO AN UNHEALTHY DIET

Colon hydrotherapy, in conjunction with the herbal cleansing program and juice fast or modified diet, successfully eliminates old mucoid fecal matter.

This is one of the benefits of internal cleansing; it very effectively removes any entrenched mucoid fecal matter as far up the colon as the cecum, the beginning of the large intestine where the water meets the ileocecal valve and then the small intestine.

Internal cleansing eliminates the toxins trapped and recycled by a sluggish colon.

Since a sluggish colon prevents proper elimination of metabolic waste by the liver and kidneys (which usually filters out poisons), this waste is reabsorbed into the bloodstream and lymphatic system. The influx of recycled waste, therefore, overworks the liver and kidneys.

Cleansing the colon, in combination with a good diet, exercise, and plenty of pure fluids, helps prevent the absorption of toxins that would otherwise enter the bloodstream through the colon wall.

A periodic colon cleansing reduces the colon wall's exposure to carcinogens.

A clean colon is vital in preventive medicine because it establishes a healthy internal environment.

Internal cleansing improves and strengthens the immune system. This is accomplished by hydrating the body, thereby improving lymph flow and by removing mucoid fecal matter and toxins. Once this is done, the body's natural immune responses to numerous illnesses are boosted.

With a healthy, intact immune system, my clients are not debilitated by weakness and fatigue as their bodies try unsuccessfully to thwart disease.

Instead, they get the benefit of renewed energy and zest for life.

How Internal Cleansing
Brought Financial Success

About two years ago I received a telephone call from a client:

Hello, Millan. I do not know if you remember me. My name is Glen, and I did an internal cleansing program from you a year ago.

I am a traveling salesman, and at that time my health was a mess. I was desperate because my sales quota was very low and my livelihood was at stake. I had absolutely no energy or enthusiasm.

I am here to tell you one year after those treatments that I have made a million dollars in sales! Millan, it is all thanks to your help and your program. Thank you!

Improved Vision

Read the following account of Bob, a client who experienced renewed eyesight:

My eyes started failing when I was thirteen years old. My prescription glasses got progressively stronger throughout high school, college, and the Navy. I am fifty-one years old now.

Always being nearsighted, I went to vision clinics for years, doing vision exercises and such. But I could not really stop my eyesight from degenerating .

I was always trying to get it to improve, but it only worsened.

I did a seven-day cleansing program two months ago and did not notice any change. Then I completed another seven-day cleansing program, a five-day cleansing program, and then another seven-day cleansing program.

After each cleanse, I tested my eyes on a home eye chart. With this last eye chart testing (wearing my glasses), everything was very blurry, and I could not figure out what was going on.

I just changed my prescription recently, and now it seems my glasses are too strong! It is just like magic! This is incredible!

Personal Testimony: Overcoming Temperature Intolerance Through Cleansing

Another client experienced a regain in body temperature regulation:

I was born and raised in California and could not tolerate really hot or very cold weather, but since my body has been cleansed I look forward to going to New York in the winter. I find extreme temperatures do not bother me as in the old days.

Randy

Therapy Stimulates Peristalsis

Colon hydrotherapy stimulates the natural mechanical action of a sluggish or "flaccid" colon to resume normal peristalsis. Colon hydrotherapy helps to tone up and exercise the colon so it can begin to take care of itself. When the large intestine is flaccid and holding mucoidal fecal matter, it cannot contract effectively. The blood supply is inhibited. Little beneficial absorption or waste elimination can happen.

When the sewage is cleaned out of this impacted muscular organ, the colon, it can begin to function efficiently again; hence, the blood supply and its vital transference functions are improved. This, in turn, improves water and mineral absorption.

Less Cellulite, No B.O., and Healthier Skin Through Internal Cleansing

Internal cleansing improved the following lady's appearance and her body's natural hygiene. Our client, Cookie, wrote to us about her experience:

Since my internal cleansing, I have noticed my cellulite has diminished, and my skin has gotten softer!

149

*Before, my skin was chalky and dull. I
have lost four pounds, which is great, and my
skin appears healthier.*

*What impressed me the most was I no
longer have body odor under my arms the way I
used to.*

*People have commented that my skin looks
great.*

I feel very good.

Body Hygiene and Internal Cleansing

Because we work and live closely together in
offices, exercise gyms, cars, buses, theaters,
restaurants, and homes, we are naturally concerned
about our body hygiene.

For better or worse, our appearance and
personal odor influence how we are perceived by our
employers, co-workers, people we do business with,
friends, lovers, and family members. Even those
people with whom we pray and worship are not
immune from the impressions of their senses.

The primary origin of offensive smells
emanating from our bodies - such as strong body
odor and bad breath - is a toxic body and sluggish
colon.

A Client Finds Relief from Impacted Colon

A severely impacted colon can press painfully
against the diaphragm and cause breathing
problems, as my client Clyde's story demonstrates:

*I used to have a tightness near my rib cage
and had problems breathing. I went to the
doctor and he said nothing was wrong, just lose
weight.*

My whole abdomen felt full.

*A series of internal cleansing sessions
moved this blockage and the tightness
disappeared. I have not had that tightness
since and it has been a year.*

Fresh-Smelling People

The profits of the multi-billion dollar cosmetic,
deodorant, and perfume industries testify to our

obsession with looking beautiful and smelling "as fresh as spring flowers."

A clean colon permits clean, natural body odors to exude from our bodies. We are a society of cleanliness and hygiene, yet we walk around with worms, parasites, and sewage in our bodies. We use perfumes and deodorant to camouflage body odors coming from within.

My clients have claimed that when their body is internally clean it is not necessary to bathe daily. Did you know that your breath could be sweet-smelling without having to brush your teeth everyday?

Did you know that the smell God intended for your body is the most pleasant odor you can imagine?

One man shared with me he had been living with a woman for a few years. He said her vagina smelled so bad he could not have sex with her. He told her so, and she went to the doctor for help. The doctor told her he could not do anything for her. He stated that was just the way her body was functioning.

How pathetic. This is a problem that could have been resolved. There are many reported cases where sexual relationships improved through the colon cleansing program.

Sexual Dysfunction

Too many women suffer unnecessary sexual dysfunction. When no physical causes are discovered, a woman is usually advised to get psychological help or to go to a sex or marriage counselor. This is humiliating when the real problem is not subconscious resistance, revulsion, or lack of technique, but is in reality a painfully impacted colon.

Modern medicine is so compartmentalized by specialty that bowel problems remain largely invisible, and may even be entirely misdiagnosed as other problems.

But what a difference internal cleansing made in one woman's sex life! This woman was diagnosed

151

with a tipped uterus, which was accurate, but her uterus was tipped because her overfull colon was leaning on it. The doctors missed the impacted colon in every case. As she tells it:

Prior to internal cleansing, doctors told me my uterus was tipped. I had constant pain in the right and lower left abdominal area. During sexual intercourse I felt pain in the back of my cervix. My husband said he could feel the wall inside the vagina. Because of my great discomfort and pain, he had to be careful not to penetrate too deeply.

After I began the dietary cleansing program with the series of internal cleansing, my husband remarked that he could not feel the pressure of the back wall with his penis anymore. And I no longer had pain during intercourse. My relationship with my husband is far more enjoyable because the pain is gone. I no longer have to cry out for him to stop.

Substitute Aphrodisiacs

Cologne and perfume were invented originally as means of masking the turn-off of a dirty body's odors; that the scents were pleasant made them a substitute aphrodisiac. Colognes, perfumes, and even alcoholic beverages were used for millennia to sweeten fetid breath from a dirty, decaying mouth, recent pungent meals, and bad digestion. Today, for the same reasons, we keep the makers of breath fresheners rolling in greenbacks and coins!

Brushing your teeth and performing optimal oral hygiene, bathing, or showering daily are good, practical, refreshing, and disease preventing activities. We know today the health benefits of a clean body, clean hands and a clean mouth. But when was the last time you bathed the inside of your body, where all the smell really originates and honestly considered your diet and exercise level?

Before   After

Final

After internal cleansing, this client's waistline and stomach area were reduced.

When my clients cleanse the inside of their bodies for the first time, they notice a difference in body odor and skin. Their breath is naturally fresh, recalling the sweet wine, apples, or peaches romantic poets rhapsodized about in their sonnets of passion and love. A client may only wear colognes or perfumes simply because the smell is pleasing, not because of a need to cover up foul odor.

We often wear make-up to hide ravaged, blemished skin showing the effects of a toxic colon. Think of all the money and time saved - for cosmetics and acne preparations are expensive! - by not having to plaster on the stuff. How much cleaner the skin can be - after all, make-up is composed of earth chemicals and pigments: concentrated dirt and different colored, finely ground rocks!

No More Potbelly!

My clients have commented on their tummies being flatter due to internal cleansing. Much of that potbelly is the result of an ill-toned colon. Even after years of rigorous dieting and exhausting strenuous exercise, that distended abdomen does not seem to disappear for many people.

When I was in my twenties, I had a little potbelly. I had a nice figure, except for this protrusion. I started dating a weight lifter at this time who developed a wheel with a handle on each side for me to use to flatten my belly.

I used it faithfully daily for three months.

My belly became as hard as a rock, but guess what? It still protruded! At that time I had a bowel movement once every three to four days; this was the reason for my potbelly.

Now I am a senior citizen, yet I eliminate one to two times daily, and my belly is flat. I have had about two hundred colon cleansing sessions over the last twenty-three years.

Internal Cleansing Restores Body's Natural Balance

Internal cleansing, promotes the colonization and growth of the proper ratio of intestinal flora. This restores the correct PH of the colon, the relationship between the acid and alkaline. This, in turn, helps to eliminate excess gas (a big relief, wouldn't you say?), keep the numbers of toxic bacteria down, and those of the toxin-reducing sort up. It promotes efficient, beneficial digestion and bowel function.

Internal cleansing counteracts the negative effects of antibiotics and environmental pollutants. It helps by reversing constipation and autotoxemia. Since internal cleansing is much more thorough than enemas, bathing the whole large intestine up to the point where it meets the small intestine at the ileocecal valve, it actually addresses the problems of initial constipation and any other accompanying problems, especially autointoxication.

Internal Cleansing as Clinical and Diagnostic Aid

Internal cleansing can be an aid in many clinical procedures now only poorly facilitated by enemas.

It is the professional opinion of Dr. Donald J. Mantell, writing in *The Nutrition and Dietary Consultant*, that internal cleansing is one of the most important "treatment modalities" available for a multitude of health problems. He advocates internal cleansing as a diagnostic tool to ascertain certain information about digestive and clinical disorders.

Internal cleansing cleans the colon, making early detection of colo-rectal cancer easier. It does this by facilitating diagnostic procedures such as sigmoidoscopy and colonoscopy, and barium X-rays.

Mantell points out that internal cleansing should be an adjunct procedure after barium diagnostics to relieve patient discomfort and to remove residual traces of radioactive fluid. This would prevent future magnified exposure to radiation, with subsequent X-rays not requiring a barium illumination.

Patients Recover Faster From Surgery

Recently, I underwent corrective surgery. Despite the severity and depth of the surgical cuts, my healing and my recovery were almost miraculous.

The doctor, my family and friends were amazed that I was able to so quickly return to work and my normal routine, without the trauma and pain the majority of surgical patients suffer.

I attribute this to a clean, detoxified body.

Teresa

Post-operative internal cleansing is especially important for patients who have general anesthesia. The bowel is usually traumatized and shuts down under a general anesthetic. In this state, it quickly becomes constipated.

Internal cleansing could help eliminate this serious problem. Likewise, lungs could clear out faster, preventing the potential for pneumonia. Internal cleansing removes excess mucus in the system, whether pre-operative or following surgical procedure.

The irony is that periodic internal cleansing and correct diet could have prevented the vast majority of surgical cases.

The Healing Crisis

Many people go through a "healing crisis." This is an experience that can be mild or intense. A healing crisis is inevitable; some experience it within hours of their first internal cleansing session, some later. It never lasts longer than twenty-four hours.

The healing crisis happens because the body is finally releasing into the blood and kidneys all the toxins and poisons it has been accumulating for years, possibly since infancy.

The healing crisis means that the body is responding to the cleansing and is unleashing all the accumulated toxins.

During this time, a patient may experience one of the following symptoms: fever, aches and pains, headaches, joint pains, pimples, boils, light-headedness, lethargy (obviously, this is simulating the feeling of sickness, and one does not feel like doing much!), weakness, insomnia or sleepiness, flu or cold symptoms, runny nose, fever, chills, sweats, nausea, or excess gas. I always remind my client that these conditions are very temporary and symptoms will leave within 24 hours followed by a feeling of well-being and excess energy.

This is all brought on because the free radicals (those little molecular marauders that age you with oxidation) and various toxins are leaving the body. It is sometimes said that a client will feel worse before feeling better - but I know that my clients do feel better, especially afterward!

I present the complete list of healing crisis symptoms so my client will become aware of what is going on if the crisis occurs. Many people are never aware of experiencing a healing crisis. If one does experience this event, I advise perseverance. This, too - pardon the pun - will pass.

The healing crisis is brought on by two things: the juice fast or modified diet and the actual physical stimulation of the internal cleansing. Most people experience similar sensations while just fasting, which is why many people object initially to the fast.

The most difficult part of a fast seems to be going without food - fighting the hunger pangs. Some clients arm themselves with an herbal arsenal to keep hunger satisfactorily curbed.

Some clients expect the healing crisis, even want it. When it happens, they will know what it signifies and they can cheer; thus when all is said and done, my clients will have taken a solid step on the road to optimum health and anti-aging.

Relaxing Bath

If a client does not experience the healing crisis right away, it just means it probably will take a little longer to detoxify, maybe two or three more

157

cleansing sessions than the usual recommendation. That is all.

A couple of steps that can be part of detoxifying are nice, relaxing epsom salt baths and abdominal wraps. After the first day of fasting or modified diet, a warm bath is just the ticket to relax all that stress away. This bath will also begin to release toxins out of the body.

The following are general guidelines that I have suggested to my clients who want to enjoy the benefits of a soothing epsom salt bath:

1. Fill the tub with comfortably warm water. It should be hot enough to last awhile, but not so hot it is uncomfortable.

2. Empty a full box of epsom salts into the water, distributing it evenly.

3. Climb in, stretch out and soak for an hour. This will open up all the skin's pores and eliminate toxins and poisons. Without even soaping, the effectiveness of this treatment can be seen in the dirty ring and dark water at the end of the bath time. All that junk was just excreted out of the body!

4. A quick, warm shower may be taken to rinse off any residue which might clog pores again.

5. After bathing and before retiring, they gather a bottle of castor oil, a roll of plastic wrap, and a heating pad.

6. They spread the castor oil on their abdomen. They wrap the plastic completely over the castor oil, then place the heating pad over their wrapped abdomen and turn it on to gentle heat for about one hour.

Relax.

The combined action of the castor oil and the heat penetrates into the intestine and softens encrusted fecal matter, loosening it from within the convolutions and pockets of the colon. This ensures removal of the encrusted matter during the next internal cleansing sessions. Some of it may even be so well softened and loosened it will begin to come out during the next natural bowel movement.

Internal cleansing Reaches Site of Parasites' Nests

Getting water to the beginning of the colon at the cecum is very important because that critical spot is where worms and parasites reside. One twenty-eight-year-old woman was sent to me by her M.D. for a series of colon cleansings, after he diagnosed that she had an infestation of two types of amoeba parasites. She can attest to the importance of this type of treatment.

The woman came in for a series of fifteen sessions. After her thirteenth session, she passed part of what possibly could have been a tapeworm. Her doctor sent it to a lab for analysis, and, sure enough, it was a beef tapeworm.

The doctor prescribed some special drugs to kill the head. He also had her continue on the colon cleansing program for the purpose of passing the entire worm and to be sure her colon was completely cleaned out. He had no idea she had this tapeworm when he sent her to me.

Another woman came to me after she coughed up what she thought was mucus but turned out to be a live worm squirming on her tongue! Still another discovered she had an infestation when, after a session, she accidentally passed a worm-filled puddle on the bathroom floor. They were alive and wiggling.

Some health authorities estimate the majority of our population harbors worms and other parasites which remain undetected.

Symptoms are identical to myriads of other ailments it is important not to establish a positive diagnosis without complete testing by professionals.

Moreover, infestation will aggravate other existing maladies. We offer special tests to detect infestations. These involve examination of stool coming out from the ninth purge, and there are other clinics specializing in this as well.

It is not the norm for us to go to the medical doctor and have stool examined for worms or parasites. Yet this is a very common problem and we do not want to face its possibility. We do not hesitate to consent to the vet's checking our animals (pets) for this condition, yet our diet is as bad as theirs. Heaven forbid if we have worms or parasites!

I remember an incident many years ago, before I knew much about good health, which occurred during a two-week trip with my family. One hour before we left, my son forgot to replug the freezer after he had disconnected it in plugging in the iron.

The freezer was full of meat of all kinds. This freezer was located in a storage room between the garage and house, closed up tight.

When we returned home, entering the enclosed garage, my husband commented, "What is that smell?"

IT WAS HORRIBLE!!! The big shock came after we opened the door to the storage room. This little room was full of flies. How did they get in when everything was closed up tight as a drum? The freezer was loaded with maggots. But from where? This meat had to have these eggs in there to begin with.

Imagine, we would have eaten this meat!

Another time, my mother took some fish out of the freezer, marinating it as it defrosted on the counter. This was going to be our dinner that evening. The fish, however, was full of worms wiggling all over it.

THIS WAS HORRIBLE, TOO!!!

Yet we think nothing of eating raw fish in the form of sushi. Do we have any idea what we are putting into our bodies? Yes, there possibly are parasites, and or eggs, in our vegetables, but you can eliminate that problem using grapefruit seed extract or hydrogen peroxide to clean vegetables.

Place 2-3 tablespoons of hydrogen peroxide in one gallon of water and soak fruit or vegetables for twenty minutes to destroy larvae and remove pesticides, chemicals, etc.

Numerous times, while administering internal cleansing, I have seen tiny worms wiggling in the anal area of my client. Itching in the anal area could be a sign of worms. It was discovered in an autopsy that a woman who had complained of severe headaches actually housed larvae in her head. An optometrist told me that once in an eye examination he saw a worm (microscopic) dash from the patient's pupil, going back behind the eyeball.

Many times a normal stool sample will not reveal worms or parasites. It would have to have a severe case in order for this condition to be diagnosed. That is because the cecum is the region of worms. Unfortunately tucked up in the hidden recesses of the bowel, the cecum is located near the appendix, which is the beginning of the colon. A stool sample taken from the ninth purge is the very best way to detect worms or parasites.

Testimonial

Dear Millan:

I am a model, age twenty-eight, and I began a cleansing program. After my fifth colon cleansing session, I passed a penny. I remember when I was six years old I swallowed that penny; it has been lodged in my colon all these years! The cleansing program flushed it out!

Christy

A Home Implant

Taking lactobacillus acidophilus and bifidus bacteria (which can be purchased from the refrigerated section at a health food store) rectally and vaginally requires that a client do the following routine:

1. Lie down on a bed; fold a thick towel under the buttocks.
2. Lubricate a syringe of a small enema bulb with Vaseline.
3. Fill with tepid distilled water, and one-quarter teaspoon acidophilus, bifidus.

I have my female clients squeeze half the contents of the bulb into their vagina first, then empty the other half into their rectum. My male clients just empty the whole contents into the rectum.

4. Lie down for two to four hours; read a book or magazine, or sleep.

Do this for five consecutive days.

This is a wonderful, stressless, unhurried way for the body to absorb the friendly bacterialflora it needs. A person will be refreshed and ready to continue a good night's sleep. This will expedite the way to optimal health and youthfulness.

Home Cleansing Program

I offer a home cleansing program to those who prefer not to go to a Colon Hydrotherapist. This is a complete package one can do in the privacy of your home. It is easy and extremely effective. The results are phenomenal. Matter will eliminate from the body that is ropy, gnarly-looking and offensive in odor. Remember, the average American has three to fifteen pounds of impurities in the body. I tell my clients that these impurities can contribute to premature death and disease.

This home cleansing program contains five different cleansing products. Of all the cleansing programs I have tried, this one is the most effective, and the easiest to do. You will be a new person after doing this program. Be sure to get plenty of rest while doing the home cleansing program. It is five days on doing the colon cleansing, taking cleansing herbs, diet of fruits and vegetables and 5 days of adding grains, legumes, raw nuts and seeds, then five days back on the cleansing program again. I give detailed instructions on the proper way to clean the colon. **For more information, please call 1-800-311-8222.**

Dr. Harvey Kellogg, founder of the Kellogg cereal company and Kellogg Sanitorium in Battle Creek, Michigan, says in his book, *Colon Hygiene*, "of the twenty-two thousand operations I have personally performed, I have never found a single normal colon."

Dr. John Christopher, a renowned herbalist, and author of *Three Day Cleansing Program* and *Mucusless Diet*, said he knew of a man who went on a cleansing program and noticed a certain type of berry coming out of his colon. After examination, the man positively identified it as one of the exotic berries he had eaten during the war on a South Sea Island twenty years earlier.

When my clients go through our cleansing program, they can expect to have a slightly full feeling. Taking place is softening of the bowel, which breaks away any old matter stashed in the pockets of the colon's walls.

After a internal cleansing session, clients should not be surprised if they do not go to the bathroom for two days following. There is no need to be alarmed or concerned.

This is normal.

And, if they do eliminate, that is great.

A Client's Story of Recovery from Herpes

I have had an active herpes condition for about nineteen years. As I get older, I break out more times each month.

Since I have started this cleansing program, I have not had any new lesions, and that has been now ten weeks.

What a blessing.

Mildred

The Urge To Defecate

How many of us have been out in a restaurant, airport, or any public place and have had the urge to defecate?

But the average person says, "No, I cannot go now." This person chooses to wait until getting home where it is more private. Elimination is just more comfortable in one's own home, rather than a public place.

It is important that when people feel the urge to have a bowel movement, they go immediately. If they do not go, then their lack of response will cause their colon not to prompt them as frequently as it has in the past.

Again, it is our culture that places us in this situation. We feel ashamed and embarrassed that someone will hear us, and we do not want to offend because of the foul odor the waste produces.

163

This retention contributes to constipation. Then, when we do go to the bathroom, we strain. Since the stool is very hard, we have two problems: constipation and hemorrhoids.

One out of every two people I see has a hemorrhoid. It is a very common condition. The quicker people learn to eliminate, the better and healthier they will be.

Also, people must be sure that when they do go to the bathroom they are not rushed. One needs to stay on the toilet until completely finished.

With some people, fifteen minutes should be allowed on the toilet. If it is difficult to go, one can take a good book, something positive like a Bible, and read it on the toilet. Before long, a person will be going regularly.

A person should go even if no urge is felt. It will happen. Sitting on the toilet at the same time daily will encourage the body to respond. We are creatures of habit. So the idea that haste makes waste in this case does not apply.

CHAPTER EIGHT

FASTING

Most people desire to stay young and healthy. Kings would give all their mighty kingdoms for eternal youth, and millionaires would give their every last penny. Ponce De Leon traveled across the world to find the fountain of youth.

Yet, before the flood recorded in the Bible, people lived to be hundreds of years old.

Why do we not have that today?

Why do we have so much pain and suffering?

I think it is within everyone's grasp to stay young and healthy. These states of well-being are available for all, no matter how rich or poor.

Putting Forth the Effort

Cleansing our bodies, then basically eating the foods God intended for us to eat is the very simple answer. Rome was not built in a day. All the years of abuse done to one's body will not be remedied with a quick fix or a pill. We have to be patient, determined, and persevere.

What is great is that the results are for everyone! Unfortunately, many people clean out their bodies and go back to old eating habits.

One client told me, "If I can't have my beer and steak, I'd rather be dead."

I saw this man only once, many years ago, and he is probably pushing up daisies right now. Another man had prostate cancer but was unwilling to give up his cigarettes and steaks. He died just recently.

You see, there is no easy way.

As my father used to say, "Anything worth while requires effort," and that especially applies to health and a youthful appearance.

There is a perfect plan for good health and longevity. Balance is required in this plan; of equal weight are a Godly diet, exercise, and a clean body.

You may have heard it said that you do not appreciate something until you do not have it. That really applies to health, vitality, and youth. We take these things for granted.

As a young teenager seeing old people, I remember thinking, "I will never look like that. Not me!"

Can you imagine the foolishness of my mind? I honestly thought I would be young forever. Come to think of it, I also thought I would never die.

Let me tell you, I never exercised a day in my life until I turned fifty. I was determined to keep a youthful figure. I always thought exercise was for those unfortunates with weight problems or something.

I hated the thought of exercise!

But look at me now! I am like the horse in the starting gate. I cannot wait to get to my aerobics class. I am here to tell you that once one has been unhealthy and sick, and then cleansed his body, how he feels and looks afterwards is more valuable than gold.

More than that, all the effort and perseverance is worth its weight in gold, ten times over. One is never the same, not ever wanting to go back to old ways. It just is not worth it.

Take control of your health. Physical perfection is for you. Do not settle for anything less. Examine all the facts and search out the truth. An informed decision is the only way.

I believe our bodies and brains are like the engines in our cars. They have either four, six, or eight spark plugs, but if operating on only two, the performance will be poor.

Likewise, our bodies are capable of functioning in a manner far superior to what we are experiencing.

What a shame.

We each are given one body, so let us take control of it, and give it what it needs, not what it wants. I am not saying we will always be squeaky clean. That is very improbable in our culture, where food is often the center of social gatherings.

When we do blow it, let us not keep on blowing it and continue eating the wrong foods. When that happens, my clients take about twelve wheat grass tablets with two glasses of distilled water or ten blue-green algae tablets with two glasses of distilled water.

This procedure flushes most bad food, so clients feel much better and soon get back on the right track again.

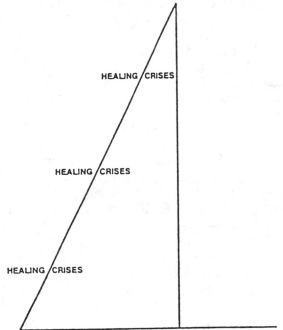

PERFECT HEALTH

HEALING / CRISES

HEALING / CRISES

HEALING / CRISES

BEGINNING OF THE CLEANSING PROGRAM

Physical Fasting

Before I went on my first fast, I used to think people who fasted would easily die of starvation or, at the least, direly damage their bodies.

Such stories are told by those who simply do not know the facts.

Yes, some of my clients experience healing crises, but that really is a good sign. As previously mentioned, this means their body is releasing toxins and poisons from the body. This process is to be expected.

I tell clients to hang in there, for it is only temporary. In truth, it will lessen in a day or two, and soon "perfect health" becomes the new goal.

In my years as a Colon Hydrotherapist, I have heard many individuals tell me they have fasted and did not do any type of colon cleansing while they did their fast of four days or more. They felt incredible illness and were miserable! I have heard this so many times. Then, the same individuals did another fast for the same duration of time, but this time cleansing their colon either with an enema or professional colon hydrotherapy. The difference on how they felt was quite amazing. They had hardly any healing crises or discomfort of any kind. I conclude it is very important to cleanse the colon while doing any fasting for any duration of time. The impurities leave the body more effectively with the greatest of ease. I'm all for the easy way!

Individuals with specific health conditions or ailments should seek out doctors knowledgeable in the area of fasting. I often hear from people, "I am hypoglycemic and, therefore, cannot fast." Or, "I get too many headaches and dizziness."

When I was in my early twenties, I would have a bowel movement only once every four or five days. Concerned, I went to the doctor, but he said for me "that was perfectly normal."

Even though I was not overweight at the time, nonetheless, I had this protruding belly. I tried everything to flatten my stomach and was very embarrassed by it. I did every abdominal exercise known, but nothing helped.

When I did my first cleanse back in 1971, doing juice fasting and herbs, only then did my tummy slim down. I am not saying this will happen to everyone, but it did happen to me. This event was truly one of the turning points in my life.

We never see the insides of our bodies, yet our internal self is key to the condition of our health. It communicates our well-being (or lack of it) in external ways - bags under our eyes, the swelling, the obesity, the quick aging, our disposition in how we treat others around us, our mood swings, our irritation at any little thing that others may say to us, our rudeness, our selfishness, our pride.

In my opinion, these symptoms could indicate a toxic body. I am healthier today than in my early twenties. I have bowel movements one to two times a day and am a senior citizen. This change could not have come about had I not made an effort. Anyone knows that constipation is a progressive condition if not dealt with.

Authorities on fasting have different opinions on what kind of fast we should do. One may say to fast on water only, but another may say juices and water only. I am an advocate of the latter, although I have done both. I feel our conditions are too toxic to deal with water fasting only.

On a water fast, the body will very rapidly release toxins from the body, which could result in a tremendous healing crisis. Headaches, fever, flu symptoms, light-headedness, and so forth could result, to the point that would make one feel extremely sick and miserable. This could be unbearable for some. For this, reason, I advocate juice fasting. Perhaps this is the reason, in the old days of supervised hospital fasts, the patient was made to stay in bed for the whole period of time.

With juice fasting my clients do not feel these symptoms as acutely. The body releases toxins, but much more slowly. They will still benefit tremendously, though.

They state that doing the juice fasting along with taking cleansing herbs and internal cleansing is absolutely the most incredible experience they will ever know. How they feel afterwards is the real evidence.

I can actually see fine lines come off my face each day! It's absolutely amazing!

Paul Bragg, in his book *Miracle of Fasting*, tells of a twenty-one-day fast he went on. On the nineteenth day of his fast, he said when he went to urinate it felt like red hot water passing through him. He had terrible pain.

He recovered the urine, had it examined, and discovered it to be filled with DDT and other pesticides. Had he stopped his fast on the eighteenth day, he would not have eliminated the DDT. It took the full nineteen days of fasting to rid his body of these poisons.

I do not recommend my clients go out and immediately start extensive fasts on their own. They begin a one-day juice fast and about one week later repeat it. Then they eat only fruits, vegetables, grains, legumes, and raw nuts and seeds. After a couple of those fasts, they can begin a supervised seven-day fast.

Going off the fast is very important. I have had clients who have done the seven-day juice fast go off with day eight eating only fruits, day nine adding vegetables, and day ten adding grains, legumes, raw nuts and seeds.

On day eleven, if they desire, they can add fish, chicken, or turkey. Taking cleansing herbs and internal cleansing is very important and beneficial during this time.

Going off a fast incorrectly can do great damage and even cause death. One case of a man, who successfully went on a thirty-day fast to shrink a tumor, came off the fast and ate a rib-eye steak and potatoes which his daughter had given him.

She was a nurse and was very worried that her father would starve to death with that length of fast. So when he went off the fast, she was ready to stuff him with this type of food.

Having consumed the meal, he died the next day.

Those with a chronic condition or a specific disease or who are on medication need to consult with a doctor who has knowledge of, and can supervise, the fasting.

I hear a lot of people say, "Oh, I could never fast, I have low blood sugar or I am borderline diabetic or hypoglycemic.

I was diagnosed with borderline diabetes in 1971 and have fasted many times with great success. I also know many people with low blood sugar who have done quite well.

Or, I hear "I get horrible headaches when I go even for a few hours without food." Yes, an individual who fasts will have headaches; yes, there will be achiness; yes, weakness and listlessness will mark the fast. I explain to my clients that when they fast, they should expect that and know the body is only ridding itself of the toxins inside. Know that it is only temporary and that it will pass within 24 hours.

Remember, fasting is not the only way to detoxify the body, but, they must remember, it is definitely the quickest and very best way to stay young and healthy.

Many of my clients will eat only fruits and vegetable two days before their internal cleansing appointment. At the same time, they are taking the cleansing herbs. Then, after their internal cleansing day, they eat only vegetables, fruits, grains (sprouted grain bread), legumes, and raw nuts and seeds.

They repeat this process either every three days or once a week. If they choose to juice fast then I recommend internal cleansing daily for the full ten days or two weeks.

Boy, what an exciting time that is! Ask any one of my clients. The results are incredible.

The reason the body starts to release impurities is because the digestive system is not functioning on a fast. Therefore, the body immediately starts to get rid of all impurities.

It requires energy for the body to remove the junk. This energy is normally used to digest food.

171

But since there is no food to digest, the process of cleansing begins.

The purification process is helped along with wonderful cleansing herbs. These herbs also remove excess mucus in the small intestines where most of the digestion takes place. It is this toxic condition together with the excess mucus in the body that hinders it from assimilating the nutrients from food.

When my clients fast, they struggle with hunger for the first seventy-two hours. But I remind them that the mind controls their body. Taking the cleansing herbs helps tremendously in controlling their hunger.

Another trick often tried is to take two rounded teaspoons of Bernard Jensen's vegetable broth with a pinch of celery salt. This is poured into a large cup of boiling-hot water. If the client likes spicy food, a few drops of Tabasco sauce may be added.

This mixture is consumed around 3:00 P.M. and again around 5:30 P.M. This kills the appetite immediately.

In *The Miracle of Fasting*, Paul Bragg tells an interesting story of hiring ten husky college athletes to take a hike with him from Furnace Creek Ranch in Death Valley to Stovepipe Wells, about thirty miles in 130 degree temperature.

The men were allowed to eat all the food they wanted, such as bread, cheese, crackers, lunch meat, hot dogs, and salt tablets.

A station wagon transported and accompanied them with this food. Bragg, who was a great-grandfather at that time, only drank room-temperature distilled water, nothing else.

The hike started around 8 a.m. The college boys gobbled the salt tablets and drank the water. At lunch time they ate ham and cheese sandwiches and drank sodas.

They all rested thirty minutes after lunch and continued the rugged hike across the hot burning sands. Pretty soon, three of these stout college boys became violently ill and vomited up their food. They got dizzy, turned pale, and became very weak. They could not continue the hike.

The hike continued with the other seven college athletes. As they continued, they drank large amounts of water and took large amounts of salt tablets. Then, suddenly, five of them got stomach cramps and became deathly ill. They also vomited and none of them could continue the hike. At about 4:00 p.m., the last two athletes collapsed and had to be rushed back for medical care.

As Bragg states, he was the only one left and felt as fresh as a daisy. He had been fasting only on water. He finished the thirty-mile hike, camped out in the desert that night, and the next day hiked back to the ranch where the hike had begun, all by himself and without any food or salt tablets.

Can you imagine, this is a great-grandfather dealing with college athletes?

I know that when I fast and cleanse my body I feel like a young, vibrant woman, with so much energy that I literally go from 6:00 a.m. to 10:00 p.m. and never stop for a break. I can do high impact aerobics and keep up with the twenty-year-olds in my aerobics class; and that is six days a week!

Thomas Edison stated, "The doctor of the future will give no medicine but will interest his patients in the care of the human frame, in diet and in the cause and prevention of disease." This is the type of doctor I am interested in visiting!

Read Up On Fasting

When a person fasts, it is important to read about cleansing and fasting. Some good books are *Become Younger*, by Dr. Norman Walker; *The Miracle of Fasting*, by Paul Bragg; and *Fasting Can Save Your Life*, by Herbert Shelton.

Extract Drink Restores Woman On Water Fast

There was a woman who went on a water fast and was becoming very weak. Against her will, she was quickly losing a lot of weight. She then started drinking an extract made of celery, beets, carrots, and potatoes.

When she began drinking it, the weight loss stopped and her energy level increased. She felt

173

much better and was able to go back to her employment while she was still fasting.

This case is another reason why I strongly feel water fasting is not the way to go. Our world is too toxic for that.

My clients who choose to take this extract drink can make it themselves. They just chop up the above ingredients and put them into a large jar filled with distilled water. The proportion is one third vegetables to two thirds water. The mixture is refrigerated overnight.

The next day, they can drink it (first stirring the vegetables), then leave it in the jar and drink it throughout the day. They make enough for four to seven glasses' worth. This is sufficient for one day's use.

Drinking Distilled Water vs. Mineral Water

In his book, *The Truth About Water*, Paul Bragg describes his personal experience with numerous watermelon flushes. He says on several occasions he ate nothing but watermelon and drank watermelon juice for ten days.

Typically during that period, he would take a sample of the first urine voided in the morning. He then would seal the container tightly and shelve it for six months to one year.

Because he is a bio-chemist, he would thoroughly analyze this substance. He found calcium and magnesium carbonate and other inorganic minerals had been expelled in this urine.

If these inorganic minerals were beneficial to the body's health, they would not be voided during any kind of cleansing. The only thing our bodies expel when cleansing are deleterious poisons.

Toxic acid crystals and inorganic minerals can cause hardening of the arteries, which leads to strokes, arthritis, heart attacks, etc.

Bragg shares a story about a man who went to a hot mineral water resort to take mineral baths. There, it was suggested he drink the mineral water because it was good for him and his body needed the minerals.

Bragg discouraged the man from drinking the water, but his advice was ignored. For six months the man drank this mineral water.

One night, during his stay at the resort, people heard him scream in agonizing pain. When they reached him, he was dead.

An autopsy showed a large kidney stone puncturing a large artery is what killed him.

I personally believe in drinking distilled water only, not spring or mineral water. There are a lot of arguments about which is better. After investigating all the pros and cons and from my own experience, I conclude in favor of distilled water.

Besides, it tastes much better than any other water. Also, it can be purchased at any grocery store. Or, better yet, one may invest in a distiller and produce home-distilled water.

People may write me, and I will be happy to direct them to where they may buy one for a reasonable price.

Those in favor of mineral water state that it has valuable minerals which are necessary for the body. But, it must be remembered, these are inorganic minerals, the same as found in dirt. If people were starving and began to eat the dirt with these inorganic minerals, they would soon die.

These minerals do not assimilate into the body for utilization. They actually do damage, in that they are deposited into the joints, gall bladder, and other parts of the body. Organic minerals are very necessary for our bodies to function well, not inorganic minerals.

Incrustation in pipes is caused by inorganic mineral water. Similarly, kidney stones are a result of drinking mineral water.

If they investigate the authorities' opinions on which water to drink (I am talking about those who themselves have researched this subject), they will find they unanimously conclude that drinking distilled water is vital to good health. For further information, read Paul Bragg's book, as mentioned above.

Many years ago, I had a class-two Pap smear, and the nurses and doctor frightened me into getting this problem treated immediately, or I would end up with cancer of the uterus.

I then went to three different gynecologists, and they all said I needed a hysterectomy. Some authorities believe eighty-five percent of all such surgeries are unnecessary. I refused to let them cut into my body, and ultimately had the area in question cauterized by another doctor. It was the most painful procedure, and my knees began to knock together as my body went into shock. After the doctor was finished, I uncontrollably began to cry. I could not explain why I was crying so violently.

About seven years later, I had another class-two Pap smear; again, the threat of ultimate cancer. This time I went on a seven-day fast, drinking only organic, fresh juices, taking cleansing herbs, and did internal cleansing each day for the week.

In the meantime, the doctor's office kept phoning me with great urgency to come in for treatment. I completed the fast, went back to the doctor, and had another pap test done.

THIS ONE CAME OUT NEGATIVE!

My doctor and nurses were shocked and, in light of the previous positive Pap smears, could not understand what had happened. I told them what I had done, and they said absolutely nothing to me. They did not even want to discuss this any further.

I provide this personal example to be an encouragement to you.

Spiritual Fasting

Fasting and prayer are two wings of the same bird. Could it be possible God does not answer certain prayers because we do not fast? That fasting gives control over the wrongs and weaknesses in life that displease God? One who has not ever fasted, has not drawn as close to God as he could.

I believe there is no closer communion, intimacy, and harmony with God, as when one is fasting.

176

We are definitely more toxic today than in Bible times; for that reason, I especially advocate starting with juice fasting.

Do not worry about observing a total fast (abstinence from all food and water); trust me, God honors a juice fast.

In Mark 2:20 Jesus says His followers will fast when He is taken away from Earth, yet in my sixteen years as a Christian I never have heard a sermon preached on the need to fast.

WHY NOT?

Millions of Jews and Christians attend houses of worship, but few are really being used of God. Why is this?

Listen, my friends, this world is quickly headed for disaster. God's wrath is close behind us.

In Joel 2:12-15, God tells us to turn to Him with fasting, weeping, and mourning - to consecrate a fast. His future wrath may even be turned into a blessing.

Nowadays, I think we all know in our hearts that worldwide destruction is inevitable, but God can, and has in the past, CHANGED HIS MIND.

Now, can you imagine yourself in obedience to God observing a fast, and, afterward, eating garbage food harmful to the body?

God forbid! This would be a quick way to kill yourself! One of the greatest writers and definitely one of the most powerful Christians ever was the Apostle Paul. How many times in his life do you think he fasted? He says in 2 Corinthians 11:22 he fasted often.

I believe that for him to write most of the New Testament as he did, Paul had to have fasted many times, just as King David did in the book of Psalms.

When one fasts for any length of time, God's Word becomes much more alive and understood.

This is powerful stuff!! Let us tap into this. I challenge you!

God says, *"And I will sow her for Myself in the land. I will have mercy on her who had not obtained mercy, and I will say to those who were not my people, 'YOU ARE MY PEOPLE!' And they shall say, YOU ARE MY GOD!'" (Hosea 2:23).*

Daniel is another man of God who fasted when making requests of his Creator. He also fasted in repentance for the sins of Israel.

Do you think we could fast in repentance for the United States of America? YES, YES, YES!

In so many sermons, church pastors tell congregations a revival is needed.

"Let's pray for a revival," they say.

Yet no revival happens. I have heard this preached many times over the years. I agree wholeheartedly this country needs a powerful revival, judging from the direction society is heading.

Why is God not allowing revival?

I have heard pastors state many reasons; however, I believe it is because Christians are not fasting in their prayer lives.

Why is this not happening?

I feel it is because Christians want to have the one fleshly pleasure that the church condones: gluttony. Does this vice not satisfy the flesh?

Spirit-filled Christians do not do drugs, smoke cigarettes, or drink alcohol, and are pretty pure excepting for the food put into their bodies. Just attend a potluck sometime, and see all kinds of garbage food with no nutritional value but simply prepared for the pleasure of the palate.

1 Corinthians 6:19 says, *"Or do you not know that your body is the temple of the Holy Spirit who is in you, whom you have from God, and you are not your own? For you were bought at a price; therefore, glorify God in your body and in your spirit which are God's."*

Isaiah 58-59 discusses the importance of the attitude of fasting, but it seems that when the Israelites fasted they were not fasting for the right reasons. They were fasting with deceit in their hearts and disobedience to God in their actions.

Evidently, the Israelites fasted, but for all the wrong reasons. They were still doing all the things which were an abomination to God. They lied, did not seek out the truth, and spoke with empty words.

178

They conceived evil and brought forth iniquity. They were also seeking out their own pleasure and were speaking their own thoughts.

I have seen the same happen today with a lot of people who come to me and are fasting. They abstain from food for all the wrong reasons, yet say they are achieving a higher level of spiritual awareness by this discipline.

I have to disagree and question what spirit they are talking about!

It says in Isaiah we need to be obedient to God, and that obedience is to feed the hungry, clothe the naked, and help the poor who are cast out. Isaiah goes on to say that then God will hear us; but, instead, people have chosen their own ways or ways of other gods.

The fast that God has chosen will loosen the bonds of wickedness, undo heavy burdens, and let the oppressed go free. This is the attitude we should have in our fasting.

One Person's Fasting Sets an Oppressed Boy Free

In his book *Only Love Can Make A Miracle*, Mahesh Chavda tells of the powerful effect his obedience to God in the area of fasting had on the life of a severely retarded teenaged boy named Stevie. Because of overwhelming self-destructive urges, Stevie had beaten his own face to the point of disfigurement. At the institution where Stevie lived, numerous measures had been taken to change his behavior, but to no avail. Stevie was tormented constantly by the other children, and he was clearly living a miserable existence.

Moved by compassion for this boy, Mahesh prayed to God for help and direction. God gave Mahesh a word of knowledge that Stevie was being influenced by a demon, much like the boy afflicted by an evil spirit was in Mark 9 of the Bible. The Lord told Mahesh the only help for Stevie was for Mahesh to fast and pray.

After fasting for two weeks, Mahesh took Stevie into a private office, told him that Jesus came to release everyone who was in bondage and that God loved him. Mahesh then called in Jesus' name for the "spirit of mutilation" to come out.

The release for Stevie was instantaneous. He visibly changed and relaxed, no longer full of tension. His self-destructive behavior never returned. As Mahesh says:

My experience with Stevie taught me a great deal. It showed me how powerful evil spirits can be in bringing illness and heartache to human beings. It showed me how much more powerful is the name of Jesus to free us from their wicked purposes. It showed me the importance of fasting, which has played a vital role in my life and ministry ever since.

Reasons for Spiritual Fasting

Why are we fasting? Are we fasting in obedience to God? Are we under some bondage or oppression? Maybe we need to fast to release or break those yokes that bind, such as gluttony or eating the wrong foods. These self-destructive habits are not pleasing to God.

Instead of seeking out our own pleasure and our own reasons for fasting, perhaps we need to fast for reasons specified in the Bible. We cannot go wrong, because God has ordained fasting. David says in Psalm 69:10, *"I have broken my spirit with fasting."*

Another thing to remember is not to broadcast a fast, running around telling everyone, "Boy, I am sure a great, spiritual person. I am on my fifth day of fasting."

I have been guilty of this myself. Are they fasting for just physical cleansing only? This does not please God.

There is no better way to draw closer to God and intimate, communal relationship than in fasting. When people fast with the right attitude, their flesh and its weaknesses diminish, and their closeness with God is magnified many times.

Talk about power in prayer!

People fast for their own spiritual awareness, a very self-centered reason for fasting. It has nothing to do with reaching out to others or doing the will of God in loving your neighbor as you love yourself, really sacrificing yourself for other people.

Such individuals do not stand up against wrongs in society. They just turn the other way and ignore their responsibility to fight for what is righteous and moral. They do not speak out against the horrors going on in our culture: child and sexual abuse, violence, sexual promiscuity, rape, etc.

Just like in Isaiah's time, there are people who fast yet are disobedient to God's laws.

In Acts, the early Christians fasted for spiritual leading and the direction God would have them go. If you are considering a job change, a ministry, a marriage, or other significant crossroad, God will give you direction when you fast. Let's really examine this #1 all time best-seller, the Bible.

In other words, what we are seeking is God's wisdom, not man's. Building a new church or synagogue, expanding a ministry, taking a trip to a mission field - when we fast and pray, He will give us direction.

This is scriptural.

In Jonah, we read where a whole city fasted and prayed, and the animals fasted as well. The king instructed everyone not to eat or drink. He also proclaimed that everyone should turn from their evil ways and the violence in their hands (That must have been a pretty bad city!).

God was going to destroy these people, yet honored the humble surrender of their bodies to Him. He relented from the disasters He had promised and changed His mind. Again, that the God of creation would do this is powerful stuff.

Would it not be wonderful if all the churches and synagogues got together to pray and fast even for one day for the United States of America? I certainly think the mighty hand of God would change the direction this nation is headed towards. This is because people themselves would be different, influencing others to obey God.

Moses fasted forty days and forty nights without food or water.

He did so on behalf of the wrongdoings of the Israelites and their disobedience to God. He requested God not to destroy Israel, and so changed God's mind.

Can you imagine? Moses would not leave that mountain until he heard from God. God answered his prayer.

It is no wonder we are not having revival. What would it take to change God's mind, considering the direction our nation is heading?

I am not saying to fast for forty days with no water, but could it be possible that if we fasted for only one day, God would honor that? Remember, he is a merciful God!

Fasting denies the flesh and brings us closer to God. It is one of the most marvelous experiences one can obtain. Sadly, I believe there are many of my Jewish friends and Christian brethren who are not participating in this spiritual discipline; then they wonder why there is no victory in the church and synagogues or in their own lives.

Diet to the Christian and Jew

Have you ever gone to church, walked up to a senior citizen, usually a seasoned Christian, and said, "Hello, and how are you today?" You need about a half-hour to hear all about their aches and pains; regretting your mistake, you were sorry you asked!

Many elderly folks are so caught up in their own physical pain and suffering they cannot be involved in any ministry or concern for their brethren. How can they be, when they themselves are hurting so much?

Usually, they are taking many prescription drugs which compound their problems; thus, they are trapped in a vicious cycle. They want to do God's will, but they simply cannot - they are too sick.

Remember the last time you were sick? You were so involved in yourself, right? You could care less about anything else. These senior citizens may claim healing from Jesus and quote all the scriptures related to healing.

Yes, in His mercy God does heal - there is no getting around that. I have seen God heal many times. I believe in the healing power of Jesus; however, I cannot and will not accept the fact God will heal us continuously when, in fact, we disobey His dietary laws.

In the Old Testament, God has given instructions regarding diet, but we ignore that. Time and again, I have talked with seniors and heard all their complaints. I may make a nutritional suggestion, and they totally ignore it and instead claim God's healing.

Did God not give His wisdom in our diet? It is a known fact Seventh-Day Adventists are the longest-living Christians because they heed their diet, for which I commend them. In contrast, it is unfortunate to see other Christians, and my Jewish friends violate God's laws in their diet.

Those laws are so applicable for today. For example, it is a scientific fact that pork, shellfish, high-fat, high-sugar, and over-processed foods harm our bodies; nevertheless, we disregard this and ask God's blessing on our food, expecting Him to respect our rebellious choices and disregard His laws.

I do not believe this is God's will for my life. I cannot and do not serve a God who expects me to grow old, sick, and in pain! Granted, I will be growing old; however, how I grow old is very important to me.

I want to grow old in a healthy manner. I want to be an asset not a burden to those around me. Look at the convalescent hospitals. What a shame that their residents are not contributing their experiences and wisdom to young people. This is a tragedy for our society.

If we would eat God-made foods, instead of man-made foods, and stop taking drugs for every ache and pain (with all of drugs' side effects), society would not have to stick its elderly away in old folks' homes, out of sight, out of mind. Go to a

183

convalescent home and look around. Smell the decay everywhere.

I want to be an asset to my grandchildren and great-grandchildren. With all the wisdom and experience God has given me, I then want to reach others way into my seventies and eighties, eventually, perhaps, even dying in my sleep.

In my old age and in obedience to God, I want be a blessing to others.

Far too many older people in churches and synagogues are not healthy. I recently had lunch with a senior whom I have known for a number of years. She is very ill with every ache and pain imaginable and is quite obese. She treats her body like a garbage can. She eats whatever tastes delicious and does not consider what is nutritious. More than that, she does not stop to consider God's laws forbidding her to eat unclean food.

This individual has been sick for two years and she is standing on the healing power of Jesus. I do not think she realizes it makes a fool out of God to think He is always going to heal when He is disobeyed.

Is not that basically the same concept we saw in the book of Isaiah when the Israelites were praying and fasting with wrong motives? God did not honor their fasts because they were in disobedience to Him.

My friend has been sick for two years and is claiming a healing, but she will not be healed if she continues to eat garbage food.

If she had cleaned up her eating habits, God would have healed her a long time ago.

She claims to be under grace, but, in effect, she is taking scripture out of context. We have to consider all of God's word, the whole of it. But we can make the Bible say just about anything we want it to, right?!

That is what the cults do!

On the other hand, I know a wonderful retired pastor named Orville Johnson, who, as a senior citizen now, is working daily down at the beaches or downtown area. He deals with the homeless, feeds the poor, ministers to these people spiritually, goes door-knocking, and just shares the love of God. He counsels those in need.

This man of God takes daily walks and my daughter says he drives like a teenager. This man is in his nineties.

His diet consists of vegetables, fruits, grains, raw nuts, seeds and legumes. He makes a nut milk (not cows milk) to put on his cereal. His mind is sharp and alert. Staying clear of pharmaceutical drugs, he prefers to take daily vitamin and mineral supplements. He has a clean colon and is vibrant and healthy.

Incidentally, Daniel 1:12-20 is an excellent illustration of the need to eat healthy foods. Daniel was under siege by the king of Babylon. This king ordered Daniel and others to eat the delicacies and drink the wine which the king himself ate.

Daniel and his friends refused, consuming only vegetables and water. They convinced the steward in charge to examine him and his friends for ten days to compare them to those who ate the king's delicacies.

Daniel and his friends physically looked better than the others; moreover, verse 17 states, *"God gave them knowledge and skill in all literature and wisdom, and Daniel had understanding in all visions and dreams."* Next, when the king called all the men in to examine their mental and physical states, he found Daniel and his three friends ten times more fit than all the magicians and astrologers in his realm.

Is this a motivator, or what?

Daniel got more than that, he got revelation about the coming messiah in detail. WOW! I do not think Daniel was expecting all that. This prayer and fasting is pretty incredible. God has given us so much, yet we have used so little.

A Testimonial

A client writes:
Dear Millan,

I had a lump about one inch in diameter on my breast. It was painful, and I became very concerned.

I then went on the fasting program, taking cleansing herbs, and doing colon hydrotherapy each day.

I am excited to tell you the lump is completely gone. Why aren't more people doing this wonderful program? I have never felt better in my life.

Millie

Dispelling A Myth About Meat-eaters

People have come to me for colon cleansing, and more than one person has told me vegetarians are much nicer and better people than meat-eaters.

This is the biggest lie I have heard!

Do not misunderstand, I am an advocate of a vegetarian diet. I believe the body is designed for a vegetarian diet, but I know some meat-eaters who are the most loving people, with more kindness and consideration for others than themselves. They are active in standing up for the injustices of this world. They are out there caring for the down and out.

On the other hand, I have seen strict vegetarians who are only into themselves, who are deceitful, dishonest, and selfish. I would trust them as far as I could throw them.

Many others have told me they are doing colon cleansing because their guru has told them this would make them better individuals. Better for whom? Themselves?

To me, a better person is one who will reach out and touch the lives of those who are suffering, who is volunteering to help the needy, to protect the child from molestation, to fight against the wrongs in the world.

Is not that real love?

I hear a lot about love. It is only a word, but love is action and that is to reach out to others and stand against the immoralities and inhumane behaviors in this world. People of love do this because they care and expect nothing in return.

186

As great as it is, colon cleansing cannot do that. A Buddhist leader who was sending all of his people to me came to me himself for colon cleansing - he said it was part of his religion. He was a very kind man and we immediately clicked.

Right away, he started witnessing to me about becoming a Buddhist and how I needed to meditate to reach a higher plain of spirituality. I told him I had reached the highest plain of spirituality when I asked Jesus to come into my heart many years ago.

"You see," I told him, "Jesus lives within my heart."

I told him there was nothing I needed to do to, except daily read the Bible, and fast and pray to God. I told him how God's Holy Spirit leads me and directs me in my daily life.

We had a very wonderful visit, and, at the end of his internal cleansing, I asked him if I could pray. He cheerfully agreed.

I then laid hands on him and the Holy Spirit filled the room. Out of my mouth poured a prayer like I had never prayed. Tears started streaming down my face and the words just flowed.

Afterwards, I looked at him and his eyes were as big as saucers. He was in total awe.

He then said something I will never forget, "You have something I do not have."

Yes, it is something colon cleansing will never give you. It is the love and power of the Almighty God of Abraham, Isaac, and Jacob.

Fasting Is Not A Weight-loss Diet

I give this word of warning to clients who have never fasted: please stay away from the scale while fasting. It can be a big enemy, especially while women fast. This can lead to a tendency of "weighing in" every day.

If one does this, as I did the first time I went on a fast, initial weight loss may be noticeable, but it is followed by slight weight gain. This is not uncommon, and, of course, it is not fat being putting on but the body is retaining fluids.

Remember, the female is the one who reproduces; this is God's way of making sure our generations continue, so He protects the woman from famine by retaining these fluids.

Despite this, getting on the scale can be very discouraging. Do not forget, however, fasting breaks the vicious cycle of craving fattening foods, eating them, gaining weight, and feeling out of control.

Yes, during fasting, fat is ultimately lost.

Also, it is important to keep in mind that muscle weighs more than fat. So, if one begins an exercise program, the scale will give the impression of weight gain, when, in actuality, one is losing ugly fat.

My advice is to let one's clothing be the guide. I know we women have to be careful to allow nothing to come along and discourage us! Finally, I warn my clients to be very careful not to overeat when they go off their fast.

A Client's Victory Over Food Cravings

Even men experience a change in their appetite for certain foods. One client, Andrew, writes:

Dear Millan:

Even after only five internal cleansing sessions in an eight-day period, I felt tremendously relieved.

My skin cleared up dramatically, bad breath, body odor, and gas have ceased, and constant cravings for various foods have lessened.

I am looking forward to getting five more treatments when I came back from Japan. I feel certain internal cleansing can benefit any individual with the desire to improve his or her state of health. It does work.

Avoiding Temptation

Some experts on fasting state the appetite (for healthy food) will return only after the body has been detoxified and cleansed. That has not been my case. It is true the appetite subsides after seventy-two hours; however, I can get hungry any time during my fasting. Everyone is different.

Before After

This client's physical appearance started to improve through a program of cleansing and fasting.

I advise my clients against watching TV, or going any place where there is food. It is recommended clients stay away from social gatherings where food is served, and even that homemakers retire into their rooms after preparing the meal for their family.

What Happens During A Fast

Reading the literature or a book on fasting during this time is very important. During a fast, the body is rebuilding cells and tissues as well as regenerating them. The enzymes and nutrients in juices consumed feed the cells and tissues, giving them nourishment. This, in turn, provides energy, well-being, and good appearance.

Testimonial of a Migraine Sufferer

Dear Millan:

I have suffered migraine headaches for quite some time. I had gone to a chiropractor for help, but to no avail.

I have gotten four internal cleansing sessions from you and did your cleansing program. I could not get any more because I am now in Chicago with my family.

I am writing to tell you my headaches are gone completely. I cannot believe it! It is so wonderful to have a normal life again!

Sincerely,
Dan

Dr. Teofilo De La Torre, in his book, *The Process of Physical Purification*, states the following:

We can compare the body to a huge sponge which is saturated with filthy water. If we want to cleanse and purify a sponge we succeed in doing so by:

1. Squeezing the sponge so that the dirty filthy water is pressed out. This corresponds to the process of fasting. During the fast the human sponge is being squeezed, thus forcing out of the body calcareous deposits, toxins, uric acid and other waste products.

190

2. Then, after the sponge has been squeezed and part of its filth forced out, if we submerge it in clean pure water, the sponge will absorb some of this water and become saturated with a cleaner and purer fluid.   But it may have taken several processes of squeezing the dirty water out of the sponge and letting it absorb clean water before we can succeed in removing all the filth from the sponge.

Equally so, it requires several processes of fasting, followed by reabsorption, of pure food, water and air, before the human sponge can be completely purified, health restored and immunity to disease acquired.   Physiological chemists have analyzed the bodies of animal and human beings who have died from starvation.   Their discoveries throw a new light on the physiological process of fasting. According to Sterling's "Principles of Human Physiology", proportions: Fat 97%, Spleen 63%, Brain and Cord 0%.   By these figures we see that when the body is deprived of food it does not consume the tissues of the body in equal proportions to maintain the body heat and physiological function. Nor do the more active tissues wear out faster, as it might be expected. The opposite is true; that is, the most active tissues are the ones that lose the least weight during the fast.   The intelligence of the body, when deprived of food, oxidizes the least useful and useless tissue first and keeps intact the most vital tissues to the last.   Thus we see that fatty tissue, being the least useful, is the one that is consumed first and in larger proportion, its loss amounting to 97%; while nerve tissue, being the most vitally important, is left intact even in persons who have starved to death. This shows that the nerves and brain are the least dependent on food to maintain their normal functions, as indicted by the fact that nerves and brain are left intact up to the time of death from starvation, as well as by the fact

191

that fasting persons preserve their clearness of mind to the time of death.

De La Torre goes on to state:

Professor Huxley of England took a family of earth worms and proceeded to feed them as they usually eat. However, in order to make the experiment, he made this exception: he took a member of the family of worms, separated it from the group and fed it in the same manner but with this exception. Professor Huxley submitted this particular worm to short periods of fasting, followed by periods of feeding on the same kind of food given to its brother worms. The results obtained were remarkable, amazing, almost miraculous. Much more so if we take into consideration the seemingly unimportant difference to which the one worm was submitted, that is, periodic fasting; otherwise, all the worms were living under the same identical conditions. Professor Huxley was very much surprised to see that the single worm submitted to the fast began to shrink in size and grow very small as the fast proceeded. But as soon as feeding was resumed the worm began to grow very rapidly, NOT AS AN OLD WORM BUT AS A YOUNG WORM. But the amazing fact was that by means of periodic fasts, Professor Huxley succeeded in maintaining the life of the worm 19 times longer than that of its brothers.

Consider the importance of this discovery. Nineteen generations springing up from brother worms had come into being, procreated, declined, and died, while this particular worm (through periodic fasting) had been rejuvenated and was very much alive when Huxley stopped the experiment.

Another observation by Huxley was that worms, animals, or even humans, if fed all the food they wanted and had no work to do, became lazy, fat, infirm, rigid, and grew old before their times.

I am not saying that we are worms; however, it has been my observation that when a person fasts periodically, life is extended and one becomes a healthy, energetic, and vivacious individual.

This experiment is certainly worth thinking about and considering.

Testimonial of Juice-fast: Overcoming Drug And Alcohol Abuse

I have a tremendous background of drug abuse. You name it, and I did it. I also drank very heavily. I am now forty years old, and I felt detoxification and internal cleansing would help me. I read about it and did a series with Millan.

With her supervision in my juice fasting, colon hydrotherapy, and taking the cleansing herbs, I was shocked to see all this sewage come out of my body. I think what really shocked me was even after my seventh session, the smell of the stool which came out of my body was wretched. It was unbelievable after that many treatments!

I am so grateful I did this cleansing program. My life and health have really improved. Thank you, Millan.

Walter

Stop Smoking - Fast!

Many of my clients who were smokers tried everything to stop smoking, then considered a cleansing fast. Clients have said when they fast, their bodies were repulsed from smoking another cigarette. The same occurs with caffeine or drugs. The desire for these substances can leave because the chemicals which cause the cravings have left, releasing the body from these habit-forming materials.

The results prove that fasting cleansed my clients' bodies and immediately does the job to get rid of the toxins, poisons, and sewage inside.

That is the reason that I feel very strongly about resting, especially the first three days of a fast. Exercise is a strong no-no. After the third day, my clients take short walks, to get the circulation and lymph moving towards elimination.

I am an advocate of fasting. I have seen time and again the benefits of fasting.

Dr. Harvey Kellogg a renowned researcher in his field, in his book, *Colon Hygiene*, discourages fasting. He states his reasons in the following passage:

Bile, mucus and other secretions as well as poisonous excretions from the blood are accumulating from day to day, but there is no peristaltic movement to carry them onward because no food is taken into the stomach. From these facts it is evident that absolute fasting is not beneficial.

I agree with Kellogg to a certain extent. When one fasts for any length of time - and I am not talking about a one-day fast, I am talking about seven days or more - taking the cleansing herbs and colon cleansing during the fast is absolutely vital. Earlier advocates of fasting also recommended cleansing herbs with colon hydrotherapy.

Did you know that when one goes without food for a period of time the stomach contracts to half its size? For this reason, a person will feel full if too much is eaten after a fast.

When I supervise a fast, I warn clients to be very careful not to overeat after properly going off their fast. They need to be very aware of this precaution. Even though they are eating God-made foods, they never should overdo it.

I tell them to listen to their body. That may sound strange, but if people are aware of the digestion process taking place in their body, they can avoid over-indulgence.

For starters, the stomach is only the size of a fist. Look at the food on the plate. How much is there? More than their fist's worth, and the stomach gets weakened by the forced enlargement.

It is impossible to fast when a person is around others who do not understand the benefits of fasting. For any long-term fast of seven days or more, professional supervision is absolutely vital. I tell my clients not to break their fast when feeling sick. Indeed, this is when the body is eliminating toxins. Rather than taking in food at this time, my clients are advised to drink lemon juice and raw honey mixed in a cup of hot water. This beverage hastens the elimination process.

Everybody is in one of the following states of health: no health, poor health, good health, or excellent health. In which condition of health are you?

Fasting Lowered Fat and Sugar Levels

Before I came to Millan for a fasting and colon cleansing program, my triglycerides and cholesterol level were high, and I was concerned. I fasted on the juices and did the colon cleansing sessions each day for seven days. I then went back to the doctor and was tested; my levels were down to normal! I feel great, and my belly went flat!

Ron

I want to share with the brethren who simply cannot go without food in their own home or environment. They have found it very difficult, with temptations all around.

There is a place for personal retreat called "Prayer Mountain." I have stayed there for seven-day fasts. In the little mountain town of Romoland, California, this retreat center truly is away from civilization. It is about 1 1/2 hours north of San Diego, about forty minutes east of Riverside, and 1 1/2 hours east of Los Angeles.

Its surroundings and living quarters are modest. It is a very peaceful place, and it has a lovely area in which to take walks. The people here glow with the love of God and are very helpful in making you comfortable. Residents are on their own though on their fast. No one takes care of them or nurses them during any healing crisis, should there be any.

At Prayer Mountain, it is just you and God.

There are no televisions, radios, or outside influence. It is very quiet there except for the unusual, soothing chirps of the beautiful peacocks that wander around. One should bring his own water, etc. It is wise to dress warm because while on a fast one can get chilled.

The price is modest. There is a public telephone. Chapel services are held three times daily, with lovely music and time for some fellowship. Attendees can expect to be blessed and draw closer to God as they never have before.

And one should not forget to bring a Bible!

Prayer Mountain is under the direction of Paul Yonggi Cho, pastor of the largest church in the world (headquartered in Korea). This church is a strong advocate of fasting (part of their church practice). At Prayer Mountain, one can expect miracles and the power of God to move in a mighty way. They do strict fasting at Prayer Mountain and do not practice any cleansing herbs or internal cleansing. They can be reached by phoning (909) 928-4415 for reservations.

Testimonial from a Marathon Runner

I followed your cleansing program and colon cleansing for two weeks. I am a ultra-marathon runner, and after completing the fasting and colon cleansing, I bulked up for another two weeks to prepare for the Western States one-hundred-mile race.

At that time, I put back on the weight I had lost during the two-week cleanse. Out of all of the runners, I came in second in that race. Of all the races I have run, I have never come that close to coming in first. I had incredible energy after my cleanse. Thank you.

Tom

CHAPTER NINE

NUTRITION AND DIET GUIDELINES

Some clients, despite eating junk foods, continue to do internal cleansing, expecting it to be a "panacea" or cure-all. While there are undeniable improvements with every series of treatments, they are not as beneficial or, obviously, as long lasting. I have one client who eats junk foods regularly, then comes in for internal cleansing.

The ultimate goal, the real reason for doing internal cleansing in the first place, is to cleanse and enable the body to assimilate more efficiently the nutrients it receives, leading to better health and longevity.

Internal cleansing is just an initial preparation for the complete program, real success, and final results. So, if individuals do not change their diet, internal cleansing can only have a limited effect on their overall well-being.

As you read earlier, bad health is largely the direct result of a bad diet. Our Western, American diet is a major reason so much ill health, unnecessary pain and suffering exist in this country. With the proper nutrition, America could be a country of radiant, vigorous, healthy people, many living well into their hundreds. I might add here that I am aware that we live longer than we did in the 1800's, but please realize that with our extended years comes poor health, pain, and sickness. Who wants to live longer under those conditions?

Simply put, our bad diet is due to a lack of whole, fresh foods - fruits, vegetables, nuts, seeds, legumes, and grains. Meat, dairy products, refined sugar, processed, chemical and preservative-laced foods are the cause of our sluggish guts, our collective colon crisis, and the rise in cancer.

In other words, if it says "enriched," one would be wise not to eat it!

Chemically Tainted Food Supply

Do you know we use more chemicals in our food than any other nation in the world? Even those chemicals that have been outlawed here are used by other countries to grow foods for export to the U.S.. We import these tainted foods, and then ingest those chemicals as well.

The foods we eat start the chain reaction of health. These foods determine how well our intestines and colon absorb nutrients and discard waste products. The types of foods in our digestive tract, and how well they move, determine the efficacy of all other body organs and tissues which maintain radiantly good health.

Basic Food Groups vs. Meat and Dairy Industry

Two of the largest and most powerful industrial lobbies in the U.S. are the American Beef Association and the American Dairy Association. American school children for decades have been brainwashed into thinking the proper four food groups were dominated in importance by meat and dairy products.

It is a cultural badge here in the "good ol' U.S.A." that Americans - particularly men - hate vegetables. For instance, former President Bush stated publicly he hated broccoli, and later had to mend fences with that vegetable's industry representatives. Still, no White House or State dinner Bush attended ever had broccoli on the menu!

And until a decade ago, the executive diet badge of honor, the domestic indicator that you had arrived at a position of success, wealth, and power was to be able to afford an ample supply of steak and lobster.

Milk was the all-American drink of youth and vigor, and is still promoted as "good for every body," while cheese is a highly desired component of the all American hamburger - the poor man's steak.

It was only recently that the Food and Drug Administration attempted to change the order of the

198

four food groups, to emphasize the importance of fruits, vegetables, grains and other plant matter. But the beef and dairy industries howled so hard and loud that the ranking of proportions for each of the food groups was compromised.

Still, it is progress, after nearly one hundred years of beef and dairy monopoly on the nation's nutritional psyche.

The point of all this is to illustrate how invested we as Americans are in a false, dangerous myth of what good nutrition is and what it means. And we are paying the tragic - and wholly preventable - price, right through the, ah, rear. Somehow, we must make a concerted public effort to change our diets for the better. Our lives are at stake!

A Psoriasis Sufferer Who Did Not Observe Proper Diet

I had a client who had terrible psoriasis. He was a younger-looking man, but he was covered with sores, all cracked and swollen. The psoriasis was all over his legs and body.

It was horrible!

He started internal cleansing, coming in once a week for sessions. He started on the cleansing diet of fruits and vegetables. However, for two days each week he added fish and chicken, and corn and rye bread to his diet. Because he could not keep to a cleansing diet and detoxify completely, the cleansing program did not benefit him as well as it could have.

Obviously, he needed to be stricter about his diet but found reasons (such as his work schedule) not to. He had a very busy and fast-moving position, working twelve hours a day in the auto industry. He married and went on a honeymoon cruise, and there went his cleansing program.

The psoriasis was not on his face. If it had been, I think he would have observed a stricter program and put everything else on hold.

Sadly, not many people properly maintain this crucial internal chain reaction of nutritious food and health, and I can list at least two reasons why:

1. We need to educate ourselves, keep up with new research study results, learn the warning signs of bad health, and consult knowledgeable health practitioners in the area of preventive medicine. We should have appropriate tests run for diagnoses, and generally take active roles in the decisions of our own health.

A first step should be to start with prevention. Grandma's old adage of "an ounce of prevention is worth a pound of cure" has no greater application than to our own health!

2. Most of us are unaware of the chain reaction - the cause and effect - of food and health. The human body is a wonderfully complex machine that over millennia has responded to changes in the environment.

This human machine is remarkably durable, able to withstand abuses both from nature and self, but, after many years, insults to its integrity manifest finally in disease and disablement.

The antidote is a nutritious diet and exercise.

While there is a latent period between what one eats and its eventual, cumulative effect on the body, without correction these effects will result in premature aging, disease, misery, and even premature death.

It is this way with diet, just as it is with smoking. Only, the health benefits of a changed diet are greater and more quickly felt, because with a good diet and internal cleansing, damaged tissues can begin to repair themselves. They may actually reverse aging and disease, something simply stopping smoking or drinking cannot do.

For example, emphysema is permanent. While it may not progress after cessation of smoking, it will not regress, or get better and disappear, either.

Evidence of our cultural proclivity for bad diet is all around us. It is a notorious fact that Americans are out of shape and lead the world in diseases such as cancer, heart attacks, and digestive

200

disturbances. These health disasters are virtually unheard of in the "undeveloped" countries. Unfortunately, when any of these populations become suddenly wealthy and begin to incorporate a Western diet into their lives, as well as a higher standard of living, these diseases begin to show up.

Obviously, something is terribly wrong with the food we eat. Yet, Western medicine ineffectively continues to treat separate, isolated symptoms of individual diseases (by specialty, no less), and ignores the root dietary causes. Our medical institutions do not adequately understand the concept of prevention, especially prevention through better nutrition. This lack of knowledge is difficult to understand, especially given the clear results of extensive studies released over the past three decades directly linking disease to diet.

For this reason, some wholistic health practitioners suspect why the established medical profession stubbornly insists on the status quo: fewer health problems will naturally mean less call for the services of doctors and specialists. In turn, there would be a resulting loss of revenues, not only for physicians, hospitals, and their personnel, but pharmaceutical companies, as well.

The pharmaceutical industry is a $1 1/2 trillion industry, whereas vitamins and minerals make up only a $4 billion market. While standard markup on vitamins is fifty percent, the pharmaceutical industry markup is 800%!

Furthermore, powerful lobbyists for the dairy, meat, and sugar industries, as well as other large food manufacturing interests, promote huge advertising campaigns with limitless funds and government subsidies, not just here in the United States but all over the world. Our government even subsidizes advertising of alcoholic products, among other things, abroad.

Meanwhile, proponents of health, prevention and proper diet struggle to make an impact in their local backyards. They do so without strong financial backing, and often with the disapproval and harassment of both the medical establishment and the government.

So, for the time being, you will have to seek good health on your own, without the help of national campaigns and in-your-face advertising.

Breaking With Traditional Diet

Admittedly, traditions and habits are hard to break; we become so used to particular foods of our families and culture. But the cheese and beef dishes of our youth could eventually cause heart attacks and hardening of the arteries. In addition, if we cling to bad toilet habits through prudery, it seems clear we are setting ourselves up for colo-rectal cancer and many other diseases.

In the long run, it is easier, wiser and kinder to our bodies and families to make wise choices for good change and health.

Capitalism and free enterprise, while the best, most equitable systems of government, make it possible, even imperative, for food businesses to cater to the tastes of the ignorant consumer rather than to the dictates of good health. Ours is a culture of pleasure. The slogan, "If it feels good, do it," may not be articulated as much as it was recently, but the philosophy certainly is fixed in our behavior. We take great pleasure in creature comforts, in how things feel.

Food gives us great pleasure, it satisfies the taste buds and is socially acceptable, moral, and legal. It is maybe the one thing we like that is not immoral or illegal! But the wrong kinds of food are still wrong for our bodies and destroy our health.

Taste is not everything.

Believe me, taste buds can adapt to healthy foods and really enjoy them. Just be patient. Persevere. With today's modern methods of processing, preserving, and packaging foods, food manufacturers can produce more food, ship it farther, and store it longer than ever before. And the industry produces ever newer foods in ever greater quantities.

Most of this food supply is killing us slowly.

Searching For Health Foods

Ironically, among modern supermarkets, stacked to the ceiling with hundreds of thousands of food offerings, only a few remote shelves stock "health foods."

Think about it. If only these foods warrant the label healthful, everything else is not.

"Healthful" foods are rare, even in the fresh produce department. Because of modern growing methods and constant tweaking of natural endowments in color, size, and taste, these "natural" foods have very little nutritional value left.

Fruits and vegetables have been altered to make them bigger, more colorful, and less prone to bruising or spoiling. Plus, they have been sprayed with chemical herbicides, pesticides, and topical preservatives.

Such unnatural changes in our food supply present unknown health hazards and rob these foods of their God-given taste.

The bottom line is, as with everything else in our material-oriented culture, the profit motive. Growers' concern over consumers' long-term health is minimal, as long as food sells at good prices. After all, everybody has to make a living, and we are living in the most advanced country, in the healthiest time, and in the wealthiest century in history, right?

The fast-food niche is the greatest offender in this crass, capitalistic scrabble for profit. With technologies that speed up production and thus multiply productivity, people live in a state of constant hurriedness - because time is money; therefore, many must eat on the run.

So, they end up eating foods less suitable for the human body's consumption than ever before in history. Worse, these foods are prepared in terribly unhealthy ways (deep-fat-frying is NOT healthy!).

Food Cravings

Does the following anonymous case sound familiar?

Before I started internal cleansing I had incredible cravings for fat foods. I put on weight. My appetite was irregular, swinging to extremes. I was craving very specific foods, but eating gave me no satisfaction. The cravings continued.

When I started internal cleansing, everything changed. My eating satisfied me. My cravings changed and my desire to eat good, healthy food became more acute.

Now, I eat only when I am truly hungry.

The makers of antacids have never had it so good, for people today are leading more dangerously unhealthy, stressful lives. It is practically a no-win, lose-lose proposition for someone in today's society to try to adjust to a healthy diet.

But, it can be done!

It just takes discipline, determination, and a desire to feel great.

Downward Spiral to Illness

This whole scenario accelerates the resultant downward spiral of illness into which most of us will fall.

Yes, our diet may yield a life span of fifty, sixty, or, perhaps, seventy years. But it will also produce painful, debilitating, and expensive ailments that now begin around age forty-five, and will plague the hapless body until death.

We all share the picture of senile, wheelchair-bound, or bedridden old-age, with the sufferer consigned and forgotten in some inadequate nursing home and awaiting a meaningless, painful, and humiliating death. These decrepit people are simply weakened by disease, decay, and a degeneration of cells and tissues of the body.

A number of years ago, I used to take little children to visit old folks in convalescent homes. So many were abandoned by their families. Many were unkind and crabby. Some were so decrepit they looked frightening! You know what they gave them for snacks? Cookies and milk...such a constipating combination. Sadly, the residents cannot say "no, thank you." They have but one choice: to eat what is given them. Perhaps this is "physical endurance," but it is certainly not living with a high quality of life. A piece of fresh fruit, or a glass of freshly squeezed juice rather than the milk and cookies, would be a healthier choice.

I saw one old woman who, in her desperation to defecate, was trying to take out stool with her fingers! Is this what we can expect in our last days? God forbid!

Chillingly, statistics may be pointing to an earlier onset of the "diseases of old age" in our society, and our expected life span may be shrinking. Bad health originating in an unhealthy colon poisoned by bad diet is the culprit.

And it is totally unnecessary!

Too many of us have resigned ourselves to the idea that age brings disease, sloth-like behavior, and disorientation. Take a look back through these pages at the testimonies of people whose lives were dramatically changed through internal cleansing and proper diet, and then at the studies cited which implicate bad diet in virtually all types of diseases. They do not have to give in to such a meaningless end. IT IS NOT NATURAL!

Folks, good health really starts with a better diet and internal cleansing. A good mental attitude and an exercise program are valuable partners in a comprehensive health program, but they do not equal the importance of eating the right foods. Eating the right foods is the number one priority for attaining and maintaining optimal health.

As you have read in these pages, many opponents of internal cleansing object to it as being "unnatural." Yes, it is unnatural to put water in the colon, but eating the diet we do, of foods laced with man-made, chemical pesticides, herbicides, hormones, and preservatives is most unnatural! Eating cooked food is also unnatural.

Our bodies were never designed to take in foods with chemicals, dyes, pesticides, synthetic hormones, preservatives, and all the rest. When we eat processed, overcooked foods, our bodies cannot digest and break down nutrients for proper assimilation.

Consequently, these foods do us harm in many ways still not fully understood by science. And if the scientific community still does not comprehend the full impact of certain food substances on the human body, do not think the makers and licensees of additives and enhancers do either!

This is how we get into health trouble.

A prescription may or may not help the sufferer; often it adds new problems. But someone who does internal cleansing enjoys improved health almost immediately. And the new lease on life is accomplished without dangerous, unknown side effects, or allergic reactions.

What is natural for us is to return to a clean, healthy, and efficient colon sustained by a healthful diet.

As with any naturally positive process, one must start by getting rid of what is wrong and then doing what is right.

The immediate response from an ailing colon to a cleansing session is very positive. In its own quiet way, a newly rejuvenated colon is the answer to all objections that internal cleansing is "unnatural."

Again I will say it: to regain health, one must start by getting rid of what is wrong and then do what is right.

Internal cleansing helps do exactly that.

Without drugs, anesthesia, knives, radiation, or chemotherapy, internal cleansing and detoxification are preemptive steps against disease - with no added harm to the body.

Testimonial of a Former Cancer Victim

Dear Millan,

I was diagnosed with prostate cancer, and I decided to go the wholistic route instead of orthodox medicine. My wife prepared me organic vegetable and fruit juices which I drank exclusively a total of thirty days.

I took cleansing herbs and did colon hydrotherapy every other day.

After thirty days, I went back to my doctor and the tests were negative. There was no sign of cancer.

I am the happiest man in the world.

Raymond

Which treatment would you rather have...internal cleansing, chemotherapy, radiation, or surgery?

Which is more unnatural?

Which one has more unnatural effects?

Which one restores a more natural state of health?

What if everyone tried internal cleansing first? What might happen?

One of my clients takes a very balanced, pragmatic view. While conceding that internal cleansing may not be natural in that birds and beasts do not practice it, he also acknowledges that internal cleansing is necessary in our society today. He knows it is difficult, nearly impossible, to avoid most harmful chemicals, preservatives, and pesticides, even with his efforts at determinedly maintaining a good diet. He points out that as long as there are unnatural, unhealthful additives in the environment, he will combat them with a harmless but effective colon cleanse, however "unnatural" it seems.

This client comes regularly to have his body cleaned and refreshed on the inside.

He has taken proactive steps to maintaining his own health - his life.

Testimonial of a Former Varicose Vein Sufferer

Dear Millan,

I had suffered in the past with puffy varicose veins. They were ugly and embarrassing.

I did your cleansing program of ten sessions.

*I am happy to report and admittedly
shocked to observe these varicose veins are no
longer puffy. Many are totally gone. Thank
you!*

Mary

After Cleansing: A Gradual Change Towards A Healthy Diet

So, where does one start on this proactive,
healthful diet?

First, of course, is that initial visit to the colon
hydrotherapist to thoroughly, internally cleanse the
body. Next, with her help and guidance, is to
completely revamp the diet and lifestyle.

Any changes must start gradually after
completion of the cleansing program.

Moderate exercise should be planned into the
day; clients are not training for a triathlon, but they
should at least walk, swim, or bicycle vigorously for
twenty to thirty minutes three to five days a week to
get the heart pumping, lungs working, and blood
circulating.

The most important aspect of lifestyle change
must be the client's new diet. Clients find when
they eat right, weight drops and cravings for the
wrong foods disappear. Dr. Gordon Tesslor, in his
book, *Lazy Person's Guide to Better Nutrition*, states
the following:

*We can successfully lose weight and keep it
off by eating vegetables, fruits, grains, liquids,
raw nuts and seeds, even dried fruit, but no
roasted nuts and seeds, which includes peanut
butter.*

*Weight will come off ever so gradually,
but, if one perseveres, it will eventually come off.
What a wonderful way to eat, not going hungry,
and yet loose weight. Exercise should be a part
of this weight loss program.*

*Foods to be included at every meal are
fresh, preferably organically grown, raw fruits,
vegetables, and fruit juices; grains (including
brown rice, oats, millet, barley, corn, wheat,
etc.); legumes (including lentils, all kinds of*

beans, black-eyed peas, split pea, garbanzos or chick peas, raw, unsalted nuts and seeds).

Roasted, salted nuts and seeds are not natural to the body, so they are not assimilated and broken down correctly. Consumption of these products results in more fat conversion.

The Immortal Cell: Carrel's Discovery

Dr. T. De La Torre, in *Man's Return to his Garden of Eden*, says the following:

In 1912 Dr. Alexis Carrel of the Rockefeller Institute took a piece of the living heart of a chicken and proceeded to experiment to see if it was possible to maintain its life apart from the chicken's body. The piece of chicken's heart is given a daily washing to remove its waste products and then is supplied with the required elements of nutrition, and it grows, it grows, it grows - it grows so fast that it is necessary to subdivide it, for it would become so large that it would become difficult to continue the experiment. This piece of chicken's heart was kept alive for over 26 years before the experiment was finally discontinued. During those 26 years the piece of a chicken's heart continued to grow without giving signs of old age or loss of vitality, while many generations of chickens came into existence, lived their allotted time and returned to the dust whence they came. Moved by the marvelous discovery: 1. that if we supply the proper environment in the form of a daily washing out of the toxic waste products accumulating in the cells, 2. and then supply the proper nutrient media it is possible to keep alive indefinitely a piece of chicken's heart, Dr. Carrel was inspired to formulate the Law of Perpetual Youth and Immortal Life in the following words: The Cell is immortal. It is merely the fluid in which it floats that degenerates. Renew this fluid at intervals, give the cells the required food to eat and, so far as we know, the pulsation of life may go on forever.

I cannot help but wonder as I write that obviously Dr. Carrel and Dr. De La Torre believed we can live forever without growing old, as they both indicated.

Where are they today in the 90's? These men were around in 1912 and Dr. De La Torre was obviously around in 1957 when his book was written. I wonder if they are still alive with the youthfulness they had then. Of course, we know this is impossible, but, nonetheless, this is something to think about.

Suppressed Emotions - Suppressed Bowel

In my experience, I have observed women to have more digestive problems than men, especially in the colon area. I believe women have a tendency to hold their feelings inside and suppress them. These emotions go right to the digestive system and hinder the bowel from proper action.

Men have a tendency to be more expressive and less emotional; therefore, they have more bowel movements, on the average, than women.

Interestingly, my clientele is pretty much fifty-fifty - men and women.

I might add, the frequency of men's bowel movements does not necessarily mean women are more toxic than men. That is not the case. Just because men's bowels move daily does not mean their bodies are clean and their colons are completely evacuated.

Such an assumption has been disproved time and again.

In primitive areas in the world, constipation is unheard of. In fact, people living in small communities and on farms and ranches have fewer digestive problems overall. Those living in the civilized world experience higher blood pressure, allergies, diabetes, arthritis, constipation, asthma - the list goes on and on.

And those of us in the field of health know this all stems primarily from unhealthy diets and toxic bowels.

We need to clean out our colon.

Be careful about eating a lot of bananas. I once instructed a client to eat only fruits and vegetables two days before his internal cleansing session. Contrary to my advice, this man went and ate bananas all day long. He became quite bound up because of all of the bananas he ate. He was really in a dilemma.

The lesson is that certain natural foods - bananas and cooked potatoes - are not easy to digest. For instance, a client should not eat potatoes thinking it is only a vegetable and nothing else; after all, their hydrotherapist told them to eat fruit and vegetables before internal cleansing, so why not?

These starches will not create a cleansing effect on the body.

Thorough Chewing Aids Digestion

It is very important to chew food completely. It seems to be a problem here in this country. We are always in such a hurry, with never enough time, so we gulp down our food and drink something to wash it down. This hinders the body from breaking down and assimilating nutrients in food and overworks the body.

Digestion begins in the mouth!

I shared with you earlier about a man who lived into his hundreds who attributed his longevity to the slow and careful chewing of food. Does this mean if we chew our food slowly we will live into our hundreds?

I honestly do not know.

It could be!

Dr. Kellogg, in *Colon Hygiene*, says:

"Cows' milk is excellent for calves to which it is naturally adapted, but for many humans it appears to behave almost as a poison. The probable cause is the very inability to digest the casein of cows' milk. Personal observation of numerous cases has convinced me that at least half of the people suffering from chronic disease cannot use cows' milk freely without serious injury.

One of the prominent symptoms arising from the use of cows' milk is a condition commonly known as biliousness. In this state, the tongue becomes coated, there is a bad taste in the mouth, the breath is foul, the bowel is inactive, and an examination of the stool shows considerable quantities of undigested casein undergoing putrefaction.

No doubt, extensive use of cows' milk, under the mistaken notion it is a valuable food for adults as well as for infants, actively increases constipation among civilized people. Putrefaction of undigested casein in the colon produces an alkaline condition which paralyzes the bowel.

A nutritional consultant shared with me that if a calf is given homogenized, pasteurized milk, from birth on, it will die before it reaches maturity.

What about the milk's additional fortified nutrients? Why would that not sustain a calf? If a calf were to die drinking store-bought milk, how can we expect our children to grow up healthy drinking the same?

My Experiences As A Breast-feeding Young Mother

When I was a young mother in the sixties, my baby was born during a time when breast-feeding was not accepted. Doctors told mothers to give their babies formula.

I was the outcast because I was the only one around nursing my baby.

I did not care.

Even though I knew little about the differences between the forms of feeding, deep within me I knew I was doing the right thing by breast-feeding my baby. I remember my in-laws thought I was disgusting, even though I was not exposing myself, or anything like that.

But my husband, mother, and father supported me. After all, my mother breastfed me!

One day, my neighbor asked if I could watch her baby for a short while. Since her three-month-

212

old baby was the same age as mine, and I do love babies, I said yes. Well, would you believe it, the moment that mother left, the baby started crying horribly.

I never let my babies cry, so this was very disturbing to me. I was beside myself as to what to do. I could tell that this baby was in extreme pain. It was colic (a condition of the digestive tract).

Finally, in desperation, I breast-fed the baby.

She calmed down almost immediately, nursed for a while, and then fell asleep. Not only was the breast milk nourishing for her, but the warmth of my body was comforting to this baby.

Another incident at that time was with a friend who was a mother also. She told me her first baby suffered so much from drinking formula (cows' milk), that he was hospitalized for three months.

How unfortunate.

Later, she was pregnant with her second baby. I pleaded with her to breast-feed the coming one, so it would not suffer like her first-born. She said she would discuss it with her doctor and see if he approved.

He told her no, that breast-feeding was dirty, unsanitary, and only animals and primitives living in the wilds did such a thing.

I, young assertive mother that I was, went and told him, "You are not a woman nor have you ever breast-fed a baby. I have! You have absolutely no right to tell any woman not to give her baby the most natural start in life as mother's milk!"

How dare he!

He just looked at me and chuckled. He was probably amused that this twenty-one-year-old woman was telling him how to be a good doctor. I mean, after all, I had no education compared to his years of medical school.

My friend had her baby shortly thereafter; sadly, one month later, that poor infant reacted so violently to cows' formula she also ended up in the hospital.

While I am talking about my experiences as a young mother, I want to share also that I had my

213

baby at home, totally natural. It was wonderful. As soon as my daughter was born I breast-fed her, laid her in her bassinet, looked at my husband, and said, "Gee, I'm hungry!" I then got out of bed, went into the kitchen, popped popcorn, and made a cup of hot chocolate. The next morning I arose and washed the bedding. (I do not recommend home delivery with your first child.)

A Diet For Internal Cleansing
I recommend to my clients a vegetarian diet. It is the best plan for my clients' health. Although occasional consumption of fish, turkey, or chicken will not cause damage, these foods are not necessary. You may even find after a time on the plant-stuffs diet that your body - your taste buds - will actually reject the taste of meat, eggs, milk, and cheese.

You may actually gag. It has happened.

You will find well-meaning but ignorant folks might blanch with concern and earnestly warn you that without animal sources of protein and calcium this will harm your body.

But that is not so. Eating fruits, vegetables, grains, legumes, and raw seeds and nuts, will give all the protein and calcium the body needs, and in superior form.

Ignorance and misinformation are the true causes of ill health.

Most foods in the diet for internal cleansing are composed of complex carbohydrates. Complex carbohydrates are high-fiber, low-calorie, and provide bulk in the digestive tract. These foods are very filling; therefore, on this diet, hunger is satisfied more quickly and completely.

Another advantage - these foods do not stay long in the digestive tract because of their high content of fiber. This roughage benefits the colon by "sweeping out with it" toxins and poisons.

And, as an added plus, fiber absorbs calories!

Overweight people will loose weight.

214

Storage of Body Fat

There is little fat on the internal cleansing diet. What there is does not convert to body fat; it is broken down and burned, not stored in fat cells for insurance against "future famine" (the reason the body stores fat).

Back in the ice ages, when our ancestors foraged for food, humans developed a means of protecting themselves against hard times.

When pickings were good (in the spring and summer), and when tribes wandered to southern, warmer climates, people ate a lot at one time, and their bodies stored the excess fat to burn in lean times (through the late autumn and winter months).

Bodies lined with fat were warmer (being insulated against the cold naturally), needed less fuel to generate warmth and burn energy in activity, and were better able to ward off disease. For centuries - in fact, until the last century - chunkiness was a sign of robust good health, joviality (because of that health), longevity (because of greater disease resistance), and wealth, (since only the wealthy could afford all the luxurious food they wanted to keep them healthy and able to compete).

As in days of old, fat in the female body is still necessary for proper menstruation and childbearing. Tradition was that fat females were revered and their likenesses worshipped and emulated because they symbolized fertility.

The Lean Lifestyle

For most of our history, until the last century, life was hard. It normally demanded great expenditures of sweaty and exhausting physical labor. This tended to keep workers too lean to sustain long life. Average life expectancy until the last century was only forty years.

We come by fat storage honorably, through hard experience stored in our genes to preserve life.

But in this century, lifestyles and diet have radically changed. Most of us in the Western world do not toil at backbreaking physical labor twelve

215

hours a day. Most lead what the generations before the 1800's - and most peoples in undeveloped countries still see as - the life of the unimaginably wealthy.

And we are fat to prove it!

This is because we eat meats and dairy products in far greater proportion to plant foods than is wise.

So, we are rich, not physically labor-intensive, fat, and dangerously unhealthy. The way to health for us in our society and its lifestyle is through plant foods and exercise.

Shortcomings of Previous Diets

There are many weight-loss diets, and if you are like me and most of America, you have tried them all. Health officials are alarmed that after two decades of fad diets, exercise programs, fashion demands, and "fat-less" foods, Americans are "returning to taste." What is more, people are making peace with the realities of human, physical bodies that were never intended to look like skin-draped skeletons.

In short, all those calorie counting diets are a pain and do not work.

Starvation and protein diets have failed totally. Ninety-five percent of those who lose weight gain it all back. Behavior modification, while proffering some good tips and recommendations, just does not meet the needs.

The isolation of radical diets is anathema to human social makeup; meals should be social, relaxing, and relationship-building affairs, shared for enjoyment. Towards that end, a healthy diet is worth the effort, and makes long life worth living. In other words, a healthy body makes life enjoyable.

Good health is attainable through internal cleansing, a good, healthful diet, and exercise. There is no calorie counting, starving, or sweating.

A clear head, a clean body inside and out, health, enjoyment, and longevity - through this program one can have it all. It may take clients a few weeks, but it does happen, and does people a lifetime of good.

The gradually restored health of the internal cleansing program seems to fly in the face of our "I want it NOW!" society, and anyone looking for "instant" results will be disappointed. But it compares favorably to the disappointing process of losing ten or twenty pounds in a month, feeling great about it, and then, in horror, seeing all the weight and more climb right back on within two weeks.

My clients experience success with this program of internal cleansing, detoxification, cleansing herbs and changed diet.

For the most part, the fruits and vegetables portion of the internal cleansing diet are handled on the client's own. Whenever possible, store-bought produce should be organically grown.

If more people demanded their grocers stock organically grown produce, then bought it from them faithfully, more grocers would make the effort to get it.

Remember, the bottom line is profit. If there is no profit in selling healthy foods, the grocer cannot be expected to stock them. The consumer must make the effort to make it profitable for the merchant.

The issue of which grains are best to eat and supplement the diet rages on; and most of us need guidance here. Certain fiber herbs can be used for bulk if need be. Rice, oats, millet, barley, and brown rice are wonderful in this capacity.

The Cleansing Herbs

Psyllium is a cleansing herb and should be used strictly when doing internal cleansing. I never recommend it as a regular fiber, but advocate its use only during this time to initially expand the colon and push old matter through. This expansion of the colon causes a slightly bloated feeling. I tell my clients this is good, and should be expected.

The psyllium forms a gel-like substance, expands the bowel slightly, and attaches onto the stool in the pockets. Liquid bentonite is then taken to detoxify the system through the alimentary canal. But psyllium taken at the recommended dosage for longer than seven days drastically loses its effectiveness.

I have seen people time and again take prescribed doses of psyllium only to clog their colons - all because they do not follow up with colon cleansing.

I recommend wheat-grass tablets or blue-green algae for fiber. Unlike psyllium, these substances never lose their effectiveness. The tablets keep the bowel doing what it should, helping it along, ensuring that nothing gets clogged in the colon.

Wheat grass tablets also contain every vitamin and mineral there is. Each pill contains eighteen of the twenty amino acids, which means it has more protein than beef. Moreover, it has twice the fiber of bran and a lot of chlorophyll. And, price for price, it cannot be beaten. Only blue-green algae compares.

The cleansing herbs my clients take, in conjunction with the overall colon cleansing program, help to remove excess mucus in the small intestine. This mucus is visible through the fluorescent view tube in the internal cleansing equipment.

In some cleansing programs, my clients undergo one round of taking the cleansing herbs - five days on and five days off - while simultaneously having colon cleansing. This regimen really gets rid of all that old sewage.

Remember, a sluggish colon goes into renewed peristalsis with the internal cleansing program (internal cleansing in combination with the modified diet or juice fast and the cleansing herbs).

This is a reason to celebrate! The colon is waking and toning up, freed like a sleeping giant.

Clients might experience slight "cramping." In no time, their newly aroused colon will settle down to business as it should, letting them know, urgently but painlessly, that they must go.

NOW!

Rejoice, do not deny it! The colon is looking out for your best interests, and knows what it is saying.

Besides, compared to the discomfort and cramping a lot of them experience while being constipated, this should be productive!

Legumes

Another new diet ingredient that one may be regarding with a wary eye is beans. I recommend eating legumes (or beans), although some health practitioners do not. Growing up, we ate a lot of beans in my family. They are a great source of protein.

But you do not want all that gas, for which beans are famous, right? Well, beans do not have to equal gas if you prepare them correctly.

For gas-less beans, I do not recommend cooking them straight from the package. This method can cause gas, bloating, and digestive problems. Beans have an excessive amount of phosphorous which is an irritant of the nerves, especially if eaten in abundance.

Here is my recipe for gas-less beans:

Sprout your legumes before you cook them, both for gaslessness and for better nutrition. For greater taste enjoyment and nutritional variety, select different kinds of dry beans and mix them together with a portion of uncooked garbanzo beans.

Fill a large jar 1/4 full with the mixed beans. Fill the jar to the top with distilled water. Let it sit overnight.

The next day, empty the water and rinse the beans. With the beans still in the jar, place it on its side.

Cover the mouth of the jar with a lightweight, porous material (I use a piece of clean, discarded pantyhose cut to size and held in place with a rubber band).

Rinse the beans three times a day for three days.

Soon, they will begin to sprout. When you see the little green sprouts shooting out of the softened beans' skins, it is time to cook them! This process has changed the chemistry of the beans, eliminating the gas problem by making them easier to digest.

And you only need to cook them for about an hour, not all day the way Grandma used to.

Sauté some chopped onions and garlic in virgin olive oil, add to the cooked beans with seasonings.

ITS DELICIOUS!

Prepared this way, the beans will not give you gas.

Enjoy!

Caffeinated Beverages

I am sad to read that caffeinated coffee is harmful to our bodies, because I, myself, drank so much of it when I was younger.

I just love to walk past coffee stores and smell the rich aroma of coffee. No one loves the taste of coffee better than I.

Unfortunately, there is no getting around it, tea and coffee are loaded with caffeine. This common substance in beverages is a poison which affects the nerves. That is why it keeps you awake and "buzzed."

According to Dr. Kellogg, in his book *Colon Hygiene*, caffeine is identical to uric acid and tannin. He states:

There is nearly three times as much uric acid in a cup of coffee as in an equal quantity of urine. Tannin is another active poison to the mucus membrane of the stomach and intestine. This results in diminished intestinal movement and constipation.

Many times people have said to me, "I have to have my cup of coffee in the morning because it causes me to have a bowel movement."

Let me tell you if you had a cup of hot water with lemon and raw honey in it, you would also go to the bathroom, for this drink would stimulate your bowels to move as well!

It is not coffee that stimulates bowels to move, it is the heat of the liquid that spurs the digestive system to start moving.

I encourage my clients to switch from the uric-acid substance of coffee in the morning to ginger tea.

This beverage is a wonderful treat for the digestion and tastes delicious. Simply grate a rounded tablespoon of fresh ginger and spoon a rounded teaspoon of raw honey into a large cup of boiling distilled water. Stir and then filter through a sieve. Drink and enjoy.

What a way to start out the day!

Treat your body well, and it will serve you well.

Again, as one centenarian said, "do everything in moderation."

Do not forget the above discussion applies to tea, because tea has caffeine in it as well. Caffeine-free herb tea with one teaspoon of raw honey is a real treat.

Begin to Restore Your Health Now!

The bad news in health is a nasty, clogged-up colon.

The good news is it can be cleaned and good health restored.

And it is not such a scary thing to do!

Almost everybody who comes to me comes back for more internal cleansing as a regular preventive, like taking their car in for required maintenance checkups. Without them, the car's warranty is no good.

Without a clean colon, one's health is no good.

Many people who were initially nervous, embarrassed, and even frightened to death at the prospect of the complete internal cleansing program got over it and come back again and again. Because of how they look and feel, they know what they are doing is for their own good.

I always try to convey to my clients my empathy, care, concern, gentleness, and even love. They know I am here to help them live long, happy, healthy, and productive lives.

So how about you?

What are you waiting for?

Contact the International Association for Colon Therapy at the address and telephone numbers on the next page and find the certified colon hydrotherapist nearest you.

International Association for Colon Therapy
2204 North West Loop 410, San Antonio, TX 78230
(210) 366-2888
To find out about our products and cleansing program,
you may write or call:
Vigil Ventures
2633 Windmill View, El Cajon, CA 92020
1-800-311-8222

MILLAN'S HOME CLEANSING PROGRAM

I believe that internal cleansing is vital to optimum health. In the past ten years, internal cleansing has been advocated by more health practitioners than ever before.

When you consider that the average American consumes 1 pound of food additives per year, and there are over 3000 toxic chemicals we are ingesting, one realizes the absolute necessity of internal cleansing.

After trying numerous cleansing programs in the thirteen years as a colon hydrotherapist, and administering over 18,000 internal cleansing sessions, I came to the conclusion that this Home Cleansing Program is absolutely the easiest, most effective procedure. The results are phenomenal and the elimination is amazing! Your energy level will increase. The results are: better assimilation of absorption of nutrients, and your immune system will be improved. Longevity and good health are just a few weeks away.

Are you aware that the average American is carrying 5 - 15 pounds of impurities in their body? I feel there is an urgency to restore your body to perfect health.

The instructional booklet explains how to correctly cleanse the colon, and includes the molotov cocktail recipe for a more effective cleanse.

There are 5 different products, each serving its own purpose in completely cleansing the inside of the body. There is a slight modification of the diet with 5 days doing the cleansing program and 5 days off, then 5 days back on the cleansing program again.

Contents of the cleansing kit include 4 separate herbal products, an easy instructional booklet, colon cleansing apparatus, and the book, *Stay Young and Healthy Through Internal Cleansing* by Millan Chessman.

Don't wait one more day, do it now!

BIBLIOGRAPHY

American Colon Therapy Association, *1994 Research Project.*

Anderson, Richard, *Cleanse & Purify Thyself,* 1988.

Aviola, Paavo, *Rejuvenation Secrets from Around the World,* Health Plus Publishers, P.O. Box 22001, Phoenix, AZ 82028, 1974.

Bragg, Paul, *Miracle of Fasting,* Health Science, Santa Barbara, CA, 1931; *Truth About Water.*

Christopher, John, M.D., *Three Day Cleansing Program and Mucusless Diet,* Springfield, Utah, 1978.

Chavda, Mahesh, *Only Love Can Make a Miracle,* 1990, Servant Publications, Ann Arbor, MI.

De la Torre, Teofilo, M.D., *Process of Physical Purification,* Costa Rica, Central America, 1957.

Ehret, Professor Arnold, *Mucusless Diet Healing System; Rational Fasting.*

Gray, Robert, *Colon Health Handbook.*

Great Smokies Laboratory.

Kellogg, John Harvey, M.D. *Colon Hygiene,* Good Health Publishing, Battle Creek, MI, 1916.

Knox, D.C., J. Glenn, Box 14412, Greenville, SC 29610-441.

Lewkovich, D.C., Gary.

Louis, David, *2201 Fascinating Facts*
Malmstromm, Dr. Crister Inged.

Mantell, M.D., Donald J., "Hydrotherapy and Its Clinical Applications," *The Nutrition and Dietary Consultant,* 1986.

Pare, Dr., Writings from 1600 A.D.

Ripley's Believe It or Not!

Shelton, Herbert M., *Fasting Can Save Your Life.*

Tesslor, Dr. Gordon, *Lazy Person's Guide to Better Nutrition.*

Waddington, M.D., Joseph, *Scientific Intestinal Irrigation and Adjuvanat Therapy.*

Walker, Norman, D.C., *Become Younger.*

Wells, William, *The Shocking Truth About Cholesterol.*

Wilkerson, Jim, KGTV Channel 10 News, April 25 - 27, 1992.

Wiltsie, M.D., James W. *Antique Colonic Machine taken from Chronic Intestinal Toxemia and its Treatment.*